SEXUAL HARASSMENT

- What It Is
- What It Isn't
- What It Does To You And
- What You Can Do About It

Joel Friedman, Ph.D.
Marcia Mobilia Boumil, J.D., LL.M.
Barbara Ewert Taylor, J.D.

Health Communications, Inc.
Deerfield Beach, Florida

Library of Congress Cataloging-in-Publication Data Number:
92-054505.

© 1992 Joel Friedman, Marcia M. Boumil, Barbara E. Taylor
ISBN 1-55874-244-1

All rights reserved. Printed in the United States of America. No part of this publication may be reproduced, stored in a retrieval system or transmitted in any form or by any means, electronic, mechanical, photcopying, recording or otherwise without the written permission of the publisher.

Publisher: Health Communications, Inc.
          3201 S.W. 15th Street
          Deerfield Beach, Florida 33442-8190

Cover design by Iris T. Slones

To Barbara, Syl and Iain.
And to each other — this project has
given us a first-hand experience of
how men and women can
work together.

The Women And Law Series

1. Sexual Harassment
2. Date Rape: The Secret Epidemic
3. Betrayal Of Trust: Sexual Exploitation
4. Women And Pornography
5. Child Support: A National Scandal

P<small>REFACE</small>

You've probably picked up this book because you have a personal interest in the subject of sexual harassment. Millions of people were stunned and captivated by the confirmation hearings of Supreme Court Justice Clarence Thomas when he was accused of sexual harassment by a former employee. The once feared and secret issue received explosive coverage in newspapers, in magazines and on television. As sexual harassment became visible, we all became more aware of how little people know about it and what to do if it happens.

Do any of the following situations sound familiar to you?

- You're up for a promotion after years of hard work and loyalty, only to find that the job you've always wanted carries a price tag you never expected: sex with the boss.
- The college professor who showered you with special attention for your willingness to participate in class now expects you to pay a price for a decent grade.
- Another girl in the office is obviously the boss's favorite. You can tell by the way he looks at her. Even though you're equally qualified, the best assignments always go to her.

- The men you work with have pin-ups of naked women hanging in the employees' lounge. They often make comments about the female anatomy and sometimes specifically about you.

What do these situations have in common? They all describe victims of sexual harassment.

Sexual harassment is by its very definition, offensive and unwelcome. More specifically, it is conduct or behavior characterized by unwanted sexual advances made in the context of a relationship of unequal power or authority. The victims of sexual harassment are usually women who are subjected to verbal comments of a sexual nature, unconsented touching and requests for sexual favors. The perpetrators of sexual harassment are usually men who, by virtue of their superior positions of authority, are able to threaten the victim (or at least make her *feel* threatened) with the loss of her job or interfere with her performance on that job by intimidation and the creation of a hostile work environment.

Does this sound familiar? If you have been a victim of sexual harassment, you might not have told anyone about it — especially not at work. Victims of sexual harassment often never do. They are often ashamed or embarrassed and probably afraid of stirring up trouble and of even losing their jobs. They are often upset and angry, feeling they have nowhere to turn.

If you are the victim of this kind of harassment, you are not alone. More than 50 percent of working women report that they have experienced some form of sexual harassment on the job. A significant percentage of that 50 percent report they felt forced to agree to the sexual demands of a superior because they feared losing their jobs or not obtaining some form of employment benefit or advantage. As a result, victims of sexual harassment often remain silent, suffering its sometimes severe consequences and saying nothing. Does this describe someone you know? Have you wondered whether there is any recourse available?

This book is intended as a resource manual for people who think they may be victims of sexual harassment, want to know more about what it is and want to know what can be done about it. This book will help sort out victims' rights and suggest both legal and practical remedies. It will also discuss the procedures to be followed in pursuing sexual harassment claims through informal and formal channels, including the court system.

Contents

Preface

1 Case History: Claire 1
Sexual Harassment: What It Is And What It Isn't 9

2 Case History: Jennifer 29
Background And Development Of Sexual
Harassment As A Legal Claim 37

3 Case History: Lorene 55
Practical Solutions, Informal And Formal
Complaints And Legal Recourse 61

4 Case History: David 77
From The Predictable To The Bizarre:
Why Sexual Harassment Occurs 85

5 Case History: Joanne 103
Looking Back: How Far Have We Come? 109

Appendix A: A Note On Sexual Harassment: What
The Federal Government Says It Is 113

Appendix B: EEOC Regional Offices 117

References 127

About The Authors 131

CASE HISTORY: Claire

Getting through college and law school was not easy. I was the first person in my family to go to college and had to get scholarships, loans and jobs in order to pay for my education. I was determined to be successful — to have a secure position and to make a lot of money. I worked hard in law school. During the day I sold cosmetics in a department store and at night attended law school. I slept little so that I could have time to study. I dated infrequently but was lucky to meet James during my third year of law school. (It takes four years to complete when you go at night.)

James worked at the same store and we were very attracted to each other. James understood my need to study for school and then for the bar exam. He was patient and gave me a lot of support. During my last year of law school, he took a job with great career potential selling computer systems for a major manufacturer. He, too, began to study a lot and also to travel. We were both busy, but when we were together, we had a wonderful time.

During my last year in school I began the process of trying to get a job with one of the major law firms in town. The recession was beginning, the economy was shrinking and jobs were hard to get. Once again, I consider that I got lucky. My hard work and dedication to be successful resulted in my being one of the few women who were at the top of the class. That year one of the firms I was most interested in happened to want to improve the gender balance among its associates. My grades were good; my recommendations were tops. I was interested in the firm and in the type of law in which they specialized, and they were interested in me. I was offered a position and I grabbed it.

Six young attorneys joined the firm that year: four men, two women, all bright, five from high-powered law schools and me. I knew I was as smart as they were but my working class family and night-school background still caused me to feel that I was not quite "as good as." I did, however, feel confident that my ability to work hard and my determination to succeed would be the equalizers. James and I were very excited about our careers and our future together.

One of the first people I met was Jonathan, a general partner and head of my department. Jonathan was 40ish, not physically prepossessing, but very intelligent, experienced and aggressive. He made it clear to the associates that within a year each would know if he or she stood a chance to become a partner in the firm. Further, he not only would have a lot to say about who would still be there in a year, but based upon his perception of an associate's capabilities and dedication, he would provide each with what he viewed as the "requisite support." I could immediately tell that Jonathan was a powerful, take-charge person.

After a short orientation period, I began to work on cases, taking assignments from several partners, Jonathan among them. He seemed to be very friendly and supportive. He was a very busy lawyer but seemed to have the time to look in on me, inquire about my progress with certain cases and offer me good counsel about professional matters. I was the typical insecure associate but I was happy to finally be making progress toward my goals. James and I continued to get along well and began to talk more specifically about the future.

I had been at the firm for about four months when I began to feel that something was changing. From time to time when I walked through the office suite, I would notice Jonathan looking at me in an unusual way. He would watch me with an intense and almost trance-like stare, and if we made eye contact, he would smile in a most peculiar way. I thought to myself that he was leering, but quickly rejected that idea, telling myself that I was over-reacting, he was just being friendly, maybe he had recognized what an exceptional lawyer I was and was acknowledging that to me. But still, I felt uncomfortable.

Around this time Jonathan became even friendlier. He would stop by my office with regularity, first standing in the doorway to chat, then he began to sit down and talk and soon he moved to coming in, closing the door and starting discussions about personal rather than professional matters. He expressed an interest in my life and wanted to know what I did when I was not at work. He told me about himself, his fiancee and his marriage plans.

He began by complimenting me on my work when the door to the office was open, but shifted to complimenting me on my appearance when the door was closed. I was growing increasingly uncomfortable as he pressed to make conversations more intimate. I began to feel scared and angry. I had never faced a situation like this before and I wanted to succeed in this job so much that I convinced myself that if I just went along with Jonathan for a little while, he would soon be married and our relationship would once again become professional. That was wishful thinking at its best, for to my chagrin, he began to ask me out for lunch, then dinner and I found it increasingly difficult to come up with excuses for not being able to go with him. Jonathan was much too smart to fool. He told me that he knew what I was doing but that he wanted to give me the benefit of the doubt because of my youth and inexperience.

He then proceeded to explain to me how things worked. He told me that he was very sexually attracted to me and on which parts of my body his attraction was focused. He told me in which parts of his body he felt the attraction and what he intended to do about it. He was very graphic and used words and images that were so obscene that I felt like gasping just thinking about them. I couldn't believe that this was happening to me. I felt weak, helpless and overwhelmed. He reminded me that he was in a position to really help my career in the firm. He could give me the best assignments and an excellent performance review — or he could not.

"Think it over," he said meaningfully. As he left the office he looked over his shoulder smiling and said, "Remember, you scratch my back and I'll scratch yours."

Over the next few weeks my life became a nightmare. I was anxious and depressed all the time, yet I couldn't show it to anyone. I couldn't sleep and had no interest in food. I snapped at people and was generally very unpleasant to be around. I was ashamed and afraid to tell James what was going on. His patience with me began to wear thin. We stopped talking and planning our future together and he seemed to drift away. I was completely preoccupied with my situation at work.

Jonathan would continue to come into my office unannounced and press me for sex. I became fearful that he would attack me right in the office. Fortunately he did not. I tried everything I could think of to make him stop. Asking him to stop seemed to cause him to press harder. When I said I would report him, he laughed. I took to no longer wearing make-up and changed the way I dressed. I thought that if I made myself unattractive, he would lose interest. Not the case. I did not know what to do and saw my dreams and hopes being dashed by this controlling, lecherous man.

As you hear my story you are no doubt saying to yourself, "Who is she kidding? She's a bright, well-trained attorney. She knows what to do. She knows there are state and federal laws that protect her from being sexually harassed at work. Why didn't she go over Jonathan's head to the managing partner? There must be more to the story than she is telling."

Yes, there is more. There is one important piece of information I left out. The firm that I worked for specialized in labor law and typically represented management in the various aspects of their relationships with their employees. While I had not as yet worked on a lot of cases, between my studies and the cases I did work on, it became clear to me that should I decide to file a grievance, either informal or formal, and even if my claims were believed (although it would be my word against his), I would still wind up being embarrassed, humiliated and without a job. Jonathan might — *might* I say — get a slap on the wrist from the old boy network. No, I was already upset enough. I couldn't face years of conflict.

What Happened?

Claire left her position as associate with this large and well-known firm. She was unemployed for over a year and spent her time looking for work and receiving psychotherapy to deal with her profound experience. She subsequently found a position with a state agency responsible for maintaining and improving the various state facilities. Her relationship with James improved but Claire was not able to move ahead with the relationship. The situation with Jonathan had such an impact on her life that for a long time she felt that her emotions were frozen and she was unable to trust men. James has since married someone else and Claire and he have remained friends.

Discussion

Claire's case presents a typical picture of *quid pro quo* sexual harassment. As she relates her story one can readily see how the perpetrator, Jonathan, almost immediately set the stage for his future behavior by informing the new, young, ambitious, but naive associates that he was a powerful superior in the position to make or break them in the firm. He then proceeded to repeatedly express his desire to have a personal and sexual relationship with Claire and that her willingness would lead to his helping her advance in the firm. He also threatened to destroy her chance for advancement should she refuse. His threats were accompanied by unwanted behavior that upset and frightened Claire. Claire's attempts to alter her appearance to make herself less attractive and her directly asking him to stop did not stop Jonathan from harassing her. Her sense of powerlessness and her increasingly disturbed emotional state led to her resigning from the firm in order to escape her harasser. Despite her legal education, her fear, upset and lack of experience prevented her from using the legal procedures and seeking the legal remedies that were available to her.

CHAPTER • ONE

Sexual Harassment – What It Is And What It Isn't

What Is Sexual Harassment?

Sexual harassment refers to conduct, typically experienced as offensive in nature, in which unwanted sexual advances are made in the context of a relationship of unequal power or authority. The victims are subjected to verbal comments of a sexual nature, unconsented touching and requests for sexual favors. The perpetrators are usually men who are in a superior position at work and who are able to threaten the victims' jobs, a promotion or some employment benefit. A single incident is usually not enough to "make a case" for sexual harassment, unless it is a violent one, but repeated acts may be. For example:

- Janet is seated at her desk and her boss, Paul, places his arm or hand on her shoulder. This may be an unconsented touching. If Janet is standing and Paul deliberately brushes any part of his body against hers, it may be harassment.
- Martha, Larry's co-worker, gets up to leave the lunchroom and Larry gets up to follow her. He walks her back to her desk and she says "Goodbye" to him. Afterwards, her repeated efforts to avoid his trailing her after lunch are ignored. This may be harassment.
- David, Lisa's boss, calls her repeatedly on the telephone or sees her in person to talk both about work-related and personal matters. He asks about her weekends, who she dates and what plans she has for vacations. Lisa tries to be abrupt and evasive within the context of the relationship but the calls and visits persist. Requests for social interactions such as dinner, drinks, movies or parties are not harassment the first time David asks (although they may indicate poor judgment), but if they are repeated and persistent, and Lisa feels obligated to respond in any way that she finds personally unpleasant, this may be harassment.

Sexual harassment was first recognized by the courts in 1977 as a legal cause of action pursuant to Title VII of the Civil Rights Act of 1964. Title VII deals specifically with discrimination in employment. How sexual harassment finally gained recognition as an unlawful form of sex discrimination is explained more fully in Chapter 2 as is the broadening scope of what the courts are willing to call sexual harassment and the approaches courts and state legislatures have been willing to consider to "right the wrongs" caused by it.

Before 1977, sexual harassment typically met with a "boys will be boys" attitude from both the courts and the organizations where the sexual harassment had occurred. Such behavior was regarded as a purely private and personal matter, not based upon sex, and not the responsibility of the organization. In other words, if men were chasing around their female co-workers or subordinates, it was not the company's fault, even if the company knew about it and even if it affected job performance.

Who among us has not seen dozens of cartoons of bosses chasing their secretaries around the desk? Everyone "knew" that the complaining women had in some way "asked for it," and men were just behaving like men. In any event, such harassment was not considered a form of sex discrimination in employment and there was no remedy for it — legal or otherwise.

Today sexual harassment is considered a violation of Title VII as set forth in the guidelines established by the Equal Employment Opportunity Commission (EEOC). While sexual harassment mainly victimizes women who work in male-dominated organizations, it has become clear that it can also be directed against men.

- Nancy pursues Stephen, a male co-worker, both by calling repeatedly, asking for assistance and physically touching him. Assuming that Stephen has asked Nancy to stop and she hasn't, she can also be charged with harassment.

Sexual harassment also typically occurs between heterosexuals. However, successful harassment cases have been brought by members of the same sex for the same type of conduct. Sexual harassment is similar to other forms of discrimination (e.g., cultural heritage, race or age) in that a non-job related individual characteristic, in this case sex, becomes the basis for hiring, continued employment, job advancement or the receipt of a work-related benefit.

Title VII refers only to the employment setting, but clearly sexual harassment can occur in other environments, for example, an educational institution where an instructor demands sexual favors from a student in return for a more desirable grade.

- Sally had struck up a friendship with her chemistry professor who always seemed helpful when she had a problem with an assignment. Later on in the semester when she was really behind, he approached her with an offer for an automatic "A" in the course if she would have sex with him. This is sexual harassment — even if she was interested and even if she acted willingly at the time.

The harmful effects of sexual harassment are not only economic. They can be (and often are) physical and psychological as well. Victims of sexual harassment often quit their jobs, give up opportunities for advancement or promotion, request transfers that inhibit their careers or even accept lesser positions.

- Julie had been harassed by her boss, Bob, for months when he was transferred to another office. He offered her a promotion including a salary increase to go with him. Julie really needed the money but declined just to end the harassment.

Certainly this leads to monetary loss at a time when women still earn significantly less than men: approximately sixty cents for every dollar that a man earns in a comparable position with a comparable education.

The psychological harm is equally compelling. Women who are prevented by sexual harassment from advancing according to their abilities and ambition often develop low self-esteem and negative attitudes about themselves.

- Sarah was less fortunate than some other women who have experienced sexual harassment. After she started being pursued by Henry, her boss, she became very disturbed, was unable to sleep or concentrate on her work, lost 18 pounds and was ultimately advised by her doctor to find a less stressful work environment to preserve her mental health.

In fact, many victims of harassment develop a variety of behavioral and psychological symptoms which, in the extreme, can lead to long-term disability and serious disruptions in their personal lives.

- Amy, after repeatedly being harassed by her boss, Peter, eventually became a poor and unmotivated worker. She was often late for work, took numerous sick days and had little pride in the job she used to love. This, of course, affects the organization's productivity and requires expensive resources to hire new employees or remotivate old ones.

Despite the existence of Title VII, many women feel they are forced to accept offensive sexual advances which they believe are simply the price they pay for entering certain institutions or professions. By the same token, many men still have difficulty understanding or believing that women suffer harm as a result of being pursued sexually at work. "So what's the harm?" they will ask, just because it is a work and not a social setting. They believe that any place is fair game. In fact, they believe that traditional sex roles cast men as aggressors, that such behavior is not offensive but usual, accepted and an expected activity regardless of where it occurs. They acknowledge there may be isolated incidents when the behavior, even by their standards, is truly offensive. They do not believe, however, that the usual male/female pursuit at work crosses the boundary to reach the level of harassment.

In many cases, the answer may be that it is not the male/female attraction or even pursuit that is offensive; it is the way in which the harassment is perpetrated that is offensive. In other cases, women simply do not appreciate being pursued against their wishes in their employment or institutional settings and feel that the pursuit impairs their job performance, their career opportunities and ultimately their well-being.

- If Jacob asks Paula, whom he meets in his apartment building, for a date, she can accept or decline. Even if he asks her repeatedly, this is not harassment. If Jacob is the boss, however, the dynamics of the situation are different. Then, whether or not they live in the same building, some of the persistent contact might constitute harassment.

- Marsha hates being asked out at work. She works at an engineering firm and does not particularly like technically-minded men. Besides, she has never had a date from work that did not end up being a disaster. After years of experience, she would just rather find her dates elsewhere and concentrate on the job at work. She recalls two former jobs that she left because of romantic relationships with co-workers that went sour and she really needs this job more than another bad relationship. When Jim, one of the engineers, asks her to lunch, she immediately declines. If he keeps asking and she notifies the employer, ultimately the company will pay the price — unless it is willing to step in.

An American Management Association survey of 524 member firms, reported in November, 1991, indicated that 52 percent of these companies have dealt with allegations of sexual harassment within the past five years. Sixty percent of the reported cases resulted in disciplinary actions against the offenders, ranging from dismissal, suspension, probation and reprimands, to job transfer. Only 19 percent of the cases were dismissed without action. The issue of sexual harassment has begun to be taken seriously. In the wake of the charges against the Supreme Court Justice Clarence Thomas during his confirmation hearings, sexual harassment has gained widespread visibility and has received increased recognition for the significant problem that it is.

What Is *Quid Pro Quo* Harassment?

The oldest form of sexual harassment and the most typical type of claims are brought under what is known in the law as *quid pro quo* harassment. From a legal point of view, unwelcome sexual advances have been made and an employee is required to submit to those demands — either as a condition of employment or because submission affects employment decisions or benefits for the individual.

- When Katie was offered an all-expenses paid business vacation to Hawaii but told that she would be sharing a room with the boss, this was *quid pro quo* harassment.
- When Allison was told that young associates were a dime a dozen and the only way to rise above the

crowd was to have sex with the boss, this was also *quid pro quo* harassment.

Such employment decisions can be positive, e.g., a promotion, or negative, e.g., being fired, depending upon the willingness of the person who is allegedly being harassed to submit to those advances.

Claims for *quid pro quo* harassment are relatively clear-cut: They require that an employee risk losing her job, a promotion or benefit of the job unless certain sexual favors are given. The more recent and less clear cut legal claims are those alleging a "hostile work environment." In such cases, the complainant must show that the atmosphere in the work (or other) environment is so uncomfortable or offensive by virtue of sexual advances, sexual requests or sexual innuendoes that it amounts to a hostile environment. The workplace must be so poisoned by an atmosphere of sexual suggestion that it becomes a hostile environment.

- Jill once worked in an office where men routinely tore out pages of *Playboy* magazine and hung them on the walls. When a new woman joined the office, she would be propositioned by all the "guys" for a date. If she was naive enough to accept, she would become the subject of scandalous rumors about what went on. Women in the office were treated as if they did not exist and comments about their dress and appearance would fly around the office as though they were objects.

The problem of hostile workplaces has been so pervasive that vast numbers of women have suffered the pain, embarrassment and humiliation for a lifetime as a consequence of their chosen careers or by virtue of their need to keep a job.

The Role Of The Courts

On the other side of the equation are the courts which so dislike being asked to monitor the workplace that they have been reluctant to find liability. This has largely been because, prior to the 1991 Amendments to the Civil Rights Act, the only available remedy, if the affected employee was still at her job, was to order employers to eliminate the hostile atmosphere — a task which the courts disliked having to perform and police. Furthermore, given the limitation of their resources, courts simply do not have the time or personnel to constantly look over employers' shoulders to see if they are carrying out remedies ordered by the court.

For example, if a court finds the environment that Jill, above, complains of to be genuinely hostile, it may order that the pictures be removed and that the women be treated with the same respect as the men. But what specifically can the court order the employees to do? And how can it tell if it has been done? The court has few resources to monitor the atmosphere of the workplace. Also, it cannot prevent a willing man from dating a willing woman — or from later talking about the date. It cannot supervise the date and it cannot control the verbal exchanges (e.g., lewd jokes and comments) or nonverbal innuendoes, either on the date or later back in the office. Nevertheless, labor experts believe that such claims are clearly the most common situations encountered, and behavioral scientists believe them to be the most devastating in terms of the victim's self-esteem and professionalism.

In the important case of *Broderick v. Ruder,* Cathy Broderick, a lawyer for the Securities and Exchange Commission (SEC), won a highly publicized hostile work environment case that shook up high level executives who thought their behavior on the job was immune from the law.

Broderick's case is compelling because of the number of unrelated incidents that she both witnessed and was subjected to as a consequence of her career with the SEC. The first time that she refused the sexual advances of her immediate supervisor at her job in New York City, he had her transferred to the Washington branch of the SEC. This was not necessarily a demotion, but for her it was an unwelcome change to a less prestigious office.

The second time she was subjected to harassment was in her new office during a work-related social event. The regional administrator made an advance to her which she, again, declined. At this point it was clear to her that she was refusing to become part of the "team" of women who were more accommodating. This time the repercussions were not immediate, except for the absence of unusual "perks" that these other employees enjoyed.

During the eventual trial, Broderick produced overwhelming evidence of secretaries, paralegals and miscellaneous employees earning long lunches, business trips, cash awards, rapid promotions and select work assignments with the only apparent qualification being that they shared a romantic relationship with the boss. Broderick, who declined to participate, received only one half-grade promotion in her first five years of employment, despite working long and hard.

Broderick initiated her complaint against the SEC by attempting to speak with the branch chief, hoping that if the situation was brought to the attention of the administration, it would be corrected. She soon discovered, however, that the situation was already well known and that "making waves" would only damage her professional reputation as well as dub her as a troublemaker.

After five years of being subjected to what Broderick considered to be appalling behavior, she filed a formal grievance with the executive director of the SEC, claiming that these office behaviors constituted a misuse of taxpayer's money and defrauded the government. While she was still on the job, an internal ethics committee investigation was launched and, prior to any determination being made, Broderick was advised that she was "subject to dismissal" on the basis of "unacceptable interactions with supervisors."

The legal process, both formal and informal, which ultimately led Broderick to the United States Court of Appeals for the District of Columbia, made her continued employment at the SEC a nightmare. Supervisors criticized her work and went out of their way to belittle her performance. Her professional judgment was repeatedly ignored. When she tried to leave the SEC, she was given bad recommendations by her supervisors. Many of her colleagues refused to interact with her. Even previously friendly co-workers feared that continued friendship with her would affect their own careers. She felt professionally helpless and personally isolated and browbeaten. She reported at times thinking that she was going crazy. Ultimately her personal life suffered as well. Broderick blames the breakup of a relationship with a man she wanted to marry on the harassment at the SEC and the emotional distress she suffered. Broderick had encouraged him to pursue securities work, but he, too, according to Broderick, became frightened by his involvement with her.

After losing her case in federal district court, Broderick ultimately prevailed in the United States Court of Appeals which found that the atmosphere at the SEC amounted to a hostile work environment. The decision was hailed as a landmark case and a victory for all working women subjected to sexual advances, requests for favors and repeated sexual innuendoes.

Cathy Broderick's case illustrates not only both forms of harassment, *quid pro quo* and hostile work environment, but also highlights another important aspect of sexual harassment claims. Victims can be third parties who are either not harassed or decline to grant sexual favors but as a result, are denied the benefits of advancement and other employment perks that are given only to those who are willing to trade sex for job benefits.

What Sexual Harassment Is Not

Apparently sexual harassment is substantially more prevalent today than even a decade ago, as well as being more visible. With the gradual increase of women entering the workforce, particularly in areas that were previously the exclusive province of men, larger numbers of women are vulnerable to harassment. Surveys of a cross section of women in both academic and work environments conclude that between 33 and 66 percent claim to have experienced some form of harassment. The data, however, is subjective and not all conduct that women as individuals consider abusive amounts to a legal claim of harassment. The legal standard, which is discussed further in the following chapters, for what constitutes harassment is changing. Courts faced with this issue are beginning to give greater attention to the alleged victim's point of view. It is clear, however, that a single incident of sexual advance or even request for a sexual favor is not harassment unless it is backed by a work-related threat.

- When Dick asked Marianne, his receptionist, to join him at a friend's party, this was not harassment. She declined and he asked again — in fact, repeatedly. This may or may not be considered sexual harassment unless or until Marianne complains and/or is made to feel that her continued employment as Dick's receptionist is dependent upon her response to his repeated requests. If his conduct is unwelcome and she comes to fear for her job as a result of her repeated refusals, this may eventually "ripen" into sexual harassment as the law sees it. What the law will almost always require, however, is that Marianne communicate to Dick that she definitely does not welcome the advances. In addition, a single sexual advance, although obnoxious to the recipient, will rarely constitute harassment — unless there is an act of real violence, such as a rape or attempted rape.

The scenario above is an example of potential *quid pro quo* harassment. What is missing is that the victim of the harassment has not yet communicated that the advances are unwelcome. In short, the harasser has not yet been told to stop. The reason for such a requirement is that the behavior in question is frequently interpreted very differently by the alleged harasser and the victim.

- Gail was new on the job and she barely knew Jim when he asked her for a date. Near the end of the date, Jim made sexual advances, and she was afraid to say no because she was afraid to lose her newly acquired job. Jim, on the other hand, thought the date was going well and that she welcomed his approaches, particularly because she gave no resistance.

Not suprisingly, a common defense is that the perpetrator did not know that his approaches were unwelcome. The most common situation arises when a reluctant employee is troubled by a supervisor's or co-worker's apparent interest but is afraid to rock the boat and indicate displeasure. Such situations then fall into a pattern of interaction wherein the man develops an attraction for a woman — real and professed — and she fends him off. However, in her reluctance to jeopardize her position (or take advantage of what job benefits he has to offer), she communicates mixed signals which lead (or appear to allow) him to continue the pursuit. This can go on for some time, creating a pattern of conduct in which the parties may genuinely experience or perceive the situation very differently. Consequently, courts require that alleged victims communicate in a realistic manner that the harassing conduct is truly unwelcome.

Once a would-be complainant has indicated her displeasure in definite terms, she must be prepared to demonstrate that the harassing conduct has unreasonably interfered with her work performance or has created a "hostile work environment."

- After several months on the job Kim claimed that Ken, a higher-up in the company, had been harassing her. She claimed that he interfered with her productivity by using company time to flirt with her and try to convince her to date him. She says that she often had to stay late to finish her work, and her concentration at times was so poor that it affected the quality of the work and her ability to get a promotion based on merit.

In this regard, complainants have been aided by a 1991 federal court of appeals decision which established that the determination of whether certain conduct amounts to harassment must be viewed from the perspective of the victim. This decision acknowledged that there may be significant differences between the way men and women experience certain conduct. For example, a woman must be concerned whether a particular advance may be a prelude to more aggressive behavior which, if not now unwelcome, may soon become so. Men who have never experienced a sexually aggressive suitor may not appreciate the apprehension that a woman may feel.

This 1991 case, which is discussed further in the next chapter, established a "reasonable woman" standard for determining when would-be harassment was sufficiently severe and pervasive to amount to a "hostile environment" type of legal claim. The perpetrator was a co-worker who professed his attraction to a woman and continued to approach her even after she repeatedly declined his advances and even complained about him to her supervisor. The lower court which initially heard the complaint dismissed it on the ground that the acts were "isolated and genuinely trivial" and thus did not amount to the persistent pattern of unwelcome behavior necessary to establish a hostile work environment. Reversing the lower court's decision, the federal court of appeals held that the severity and pervasiveness of the unwelcome conduct had to be viewed from the perspective of the recipient — here, the woman.

The question of how severe and how pervasive the unwelcome sexual advances must be is more uncertain in the context of a hostile work environment suit. Since, by definition, there is not a requested *quid pro quo* (sex in enchange for advancement or salary increase) and the harasser is often a co-worker, the victim must establish a pattern of persistent and unwelcome approaches of a sexual nature which a reasonable person would react to as abusive.

So how much is too much? Repeated requests for social interactions are, by themselves, insufficient — even if they are consistently declined. To the extent that a complainant is not clear about her refusals, her case will be even more problematic. What if the parties interact socially at work but she declines his invitiations "after hours"? Again, she must clearly define and express the boundaries between welcome and unwelcome behavior.

Obligations Of The Employer

Under the law employers do not become liable until they have (or should have) *knowledge of the harassment* and *do not* act at all or do not act in a way "reasonably calculated to end the harassment." In some cases, this may mean terminating the offending employee. In other cases, a reprimand, probation or warning that further conduct will result in stern measures may be appropriate. In any event, Title VII requires something more than a "mere request to refrain from discriminatory conduct." The intent of the court in the case above was, among other things, to send a clear message to employers that not taking adequate measures to end genuine harassment could potentially subject them to legal consequences and compensation to the victim.

The type of conduct which an employer must eliminate is established in guidelines set by the Equal Employment Opportunity Commission (EEOC). The requested exchange of sexual favors for employment, promotions, salary increases — or any other employment benefit (i.e., *quid pro quo* harassment) — must be eliminated.

The objectionable conduct which might ultimately constitute a hostile or offensive work environment is less clearcut. Examples include a man touching a woman with his hands or pressing or brushing any other parts of his body against her; making a sexual advance to a woman or unwelcome "dirty" jokes or jokes of a sexual nature; displaying pornographic pictures in the office or in general, commenting in a sexual nature or making requests for sexual favors. Once the presence of a hostile environment is verified, it is the responsibility of the employer to take the necessary steps to eliminate it.

Under the EEOC guidelines, the liability of an employer depends on the nature of the conduct, the degree of offensiveness and usually a determination of whether it was consensual. The question of whether the employer had notice of any pattern of harassment is considered as well as what measures — if any — were taken to eliminate the offensive conduct.

The EEOC has also issued guidelines on the obligations of an employer to eliminate sexual favoritism. This is a potential claim by a third party who is not herself the subject of harassment but an indirect victim by virtue of being deprived of a benefit that a willing participant gained by submitting to the sexual demands of a supervisor. Under the EEOC guidelines, the liability of the employer again depends upon the nature and degree of the conduct. For example, an isolated incident of consensual sex will probably not give rise to a complaint by other employees, even though the EEOC does not define what it means by an "isolated incident."

When favoritism results from coerced sexual activity, the EEOC position is much clearer and the court is apt to come down harder on employers who knew or should have known that such practices existed within their workplace. According to the EEOC, if an employee submits to sexual demands through coercion, other employees who do not receive the benefit may have a claim against the employers for sexual discrimination by virtue of the fact that by allowing such practices to occur they "participated" in unlawful employment discrimination. In fact, both men and women who were equally qualified for the job may have a claim that they suffered a detriment by virtue of the discrimination. This type of situation has been compared to the affirmative action situation in which non-minority applicants who are denied positions in favor of a less qualified minority member under some sort of affirmative action have been allowed to challenge such practices on the basis that the non-minorities are injured by such discrimination. Denial of benefits to third parties and the resulting granting of those benefits to the targeted individual (or individuals) may not be based solely on criteria not related to job performance.

This area of the law is still developing. EEOC guidelines are relatively new and their potential implications for employers are still not clear. What is certain is that employers should have available for all employees explicit guidelines on sexual harassment clearly stating what types of conduct are prohibited. How explicit these guidelines should be is really a matter of common sense. Employers in doubt on this issue should ask themselves: How much do you wish to protect yourself against potential employment discrimination liability?

Employers should outline the rights and remedies both of employees who are approached with sexual advances and of those who believe that they have been denied a benefit by such conduct directed at a fellow employee who has taken advantage of it. Finally, the employer should have in place a concrete mechanism of investigation and consequences which the employees believe to be a realistic and reliable means of recourse.

- Jane worked for Amzar Corporation in the late 1970s. She claims that she was harassed by several of the corporate executives over a three-year period. Eventually, she went to one of the vice-presidents, complained about the harassment and threatened to leave. The vice-president responded that it was "impossible" that the men she identified were harassing her. He claimed to have known them well and was certain that she must have misunderstood them. He did agree to check out the situation and get back to her, but she never heard from him and the harassment continued.

Much has changed since the 1970s, but management and staff alike must know that the company is prepared to follow through with complaints and fire, suspend, reprimand or do whatever is necessary to put an end to the sexual harassment in the workplace. Companies that do not take this issue seriously will increasingly find themselves faced with expensive and time-consuming litigation, costly settlements and damaged reputations.

CASE HISTORY: Jennifer

I am a 23-year-old woman from a middle-class Spanish-American family raised in the Midwest. The family values are education, hard work and achievement. I am the youngest of four children with three older brothers. Being single, I live at home with my mother and two of my brothers. My father passed away four years ago. My oldest brother is married and lives in Texas.

I graduated from high school four years ago and earned an Associate of Arts (two-year) degree from a local college two years ago. My first job was as a bank teller in a neighborhood branch savings bank. Before that I had no significant employment history other than occasional work in my father's business. I stayed with the bank for nearly two years and left three months ago seeking greater opportunity to meet people and to advance in a career. I perceived, I believe rightly, that there was little opportunity to advance in that position without futher academic credentials.

My current position came after approximately a month and a half of applications and interviews. I was hired as a billing clerk at a major hospital and was promised substantial opportunity for advancement within the department which handled credit and collection. When interviewing with my immediate supervisor, Ken W., I was assured that there were many opportunities for "a woman with my attributes and ambition." I was a bit puzzled by his comments but did not inquire further and was grateful to be complimented on my accomplishments. Throughout most of my job-searching efforts I had been told that my Associate's degree was inadequate and that without a Bachelor's degree, my prospects for advancing beyond a secretarial or clerical position were grim. With little desire to return to school and no specific academic direction, I was grateful for a position with some hope of advancement.

Within days of joining the hospital, Ken, a single man of age 35, began commenting on my personal appearance. His comments were both positive and personal. For example, he suggested that a woman with such attractive legs should not hide them behind such long skirts. He also commented that although pants were acceptable in the office, skirts created a more professional image and were more becoming to me. I was not offended by his comments and, indeed, appreciated the special attention which I viewed as "paternal." I also took a personal liking to Ken, admiring his jovial personality, his sophistication concerning business and his attention to personal matters.

Although I found Ken likable and attractive, I never dreamed he could be interested in me. When at the end of the second week on the job he invited me to have a drink after work, I was both surprised and flustered. I accepted reluctantly, not out of any kind of fear or animosity, but because of my father's strict admonition (directed mostly at my brothers) about dating co-workers. He would have been strongly opposed to even a casual date. Ironically, I had accepted the job at a major hospital in part to enhance my social life but never imagined getting involved with my own supervisor.

During that first date after work, Ken's interest in me was obvious. He complimented my dress and my personality. He also commented on my bright future at the hospital at a time when job opportunities were scarce. In fact, he said that he was grooming me for an upcoming opening as Senior Billing Clerk. Such an immediate promotion exceeded my greatest expectations. More money, more status and an opportunity to demonstrate to my achievement-oriented family that I also could excel. My subtle resentment of my ambitious and more successful brothers was apparently not so subtle. This was my opportunity to be someone other than the baby girl of the family.

Something, however, was not quite right. Ken's adoration of my beauty and my business talents was excessive. I had only been on the job for two weeks and was barely trained. How could he be so certain that I would be an achiever? Why was he so sure that I could even master my own responsibilities? Besides, while I considered myself attractive, I certainly did not expect to win any beauty contests. So why all the attention? After a couple hours of too many drinks, I declined dinner on the basis of a prior commitment. I found my own way home and spent the weekend somewhat confused but wondering if this was my big opportunity to get ahead. My deceased father's wisdom weighed heavily on my mind. So did my skepticism about Ken's sincerity.

Over the next week, Ken expressed increased interest in me. He praised my work and admired my appearance. However, when Ken asked me for a second date, he apparently did not expect that I might turn him down. Although still a little intrigued by his interest in me, I nevertheless declined his invitation on the basis of not wanting to interfere with our working relationship. Ken initially appeared stunned at my rejection, but later showed annoyance with my seemingly arbitrary refusal.

Ken kept some distance from me for a few days before calling me into his office for a private meeting. His manner was casual, relaxed and friendly. He reminded me that prior to this job I had been unemployed for more than six weeks. He also commented on the scarcity of "decent" jobs available to a woman without a Bachelor's degree. Indeed he suggested that he had offered me a rare opportunity and might even be prepared to advance me. So why, he wanted to know, was I so stubborn about my decision not to date at the office? I was feeling the pressure and I agreed to re-think my position.

Over the next several days my resolve to resist Ken's advances waffled. If he were sincerely interested in me, why was his courtship threatening my job? What I once thought was acknowledgment and support, I now experienced as aggression and coercion. But Ken was in a position to really help me out.

Ken's next invitation followed only days after our meeting. He confronted me when he asked me to deliver a file to his office. For the first time he was physically suggestive, putting his arm around my shoulders and inviting me to sit on his lap. I remained rigid and reluctant and spoke to him from the opposite side of his desk. His conversation became explicit and he asked me about my relationships and sexual escapades. He asked me if I was ready to play by his rules. With characteristic coolness, he reminded me that the senior clerical position would be available shortly. Feeling pressured and coerced, I agreed reluctantly and exited abruptly.

Near the end of the day Ken stopped by my desk and suggested that I wait until the other office girls went home and he would come by and see me. As the end of the day approached, I became increasingly scared and upset. I didn't know exactly what to expect, but all I could think was that I really wanted this job. I was so distracted that I couldn't do my work and as my co-workers started to leave, I felt sick to my stomach.

Almost as though he were watching, Ken appeared at my desk within moments of the office emptying out. If I were thinking about backing out (I was too confused to know what I was thinking), it was too late. Ken said absolutely nothing to me but took my hand and led me out the door. The silence was awful and I again wondered if the job was worth it.

We walked down the street and within minutes arrived at some sort of hotel which I never even knew existed. It was dusk and the lighting inside was poor. We never even checked in but went directly to a first floor room. Ken never said a word, but his manner was cool and deliberate. This man knew what he was doing.

Do I need to tell you what happened next? Yes, we had sex, or at least he did. If you've ever wondered about the difference between love-making and sex, you should meet Ken. Eventually I got dressed and went home feeling strange and ambivalent. I was still sick to my stomach.

This scenario repeated itself at least a couple of times a week for many weeks. The weirdest part about it was that we never talked and in the office you would never have known that Ken even noticed me. The attention stopped. The compliments stopped. But the sex continued. And as promised, when the senior clerical position was announced, I didn't even have to apply for it. It was mine.

Not a single day went by that I didn't wonder whether it was worth it. I wanted the job badly but the price was taking its toll in every aspect of my life. I was losing sleep, losing weight and didn't dare to have a real relationship with anybody. What I once hoped might be a road to success now looked like a dead end. And just when I thought things were really bad, they got worse.

What Happened?

The two billing clerks in the office who had

greatest seniority filed a complaint with the hospital when Jennifer got the senior clerical position. Apparently Ken had offered them the same opportunity for advancement when they first joined the office. They had resisted his advances and were now suspicious about Jennifer's promotion. Before the internal investigation began, Jennifer sought employment elsewhere. While she was the original victim of sexual harassment, the complainants who were not promoted became the real victims of discrimination.

Discussion

Jennifer's case is not representative of sexual harassment, but rather of sexual favoritism. Jennifer was indeed coerced into submitting to her supervisor's sexual advances but despite her disgust and upset she was sufficiently driven by her own ambition and need for a high status job to go along with his sexual demands. She was given a promotion even though she lacked the qualifications, seniority or other qualities based upon performance. She delivered sexual favors and he delivered a promotion. While Jennifer was coerced, she never complained or filed a grievance. She never even said no. The effect of her promotion was to prevent other employees who were equally or more qualified from being considered for the promotion. In cases like that of Jennifer, both men and women who are qualified for the particular job benefit, in this case promotion, can claim sex discrimination on the grounds that they were injured as a result of favoritism. This case demonstrates that the law not only protects the rights of the employee to whom advances are made but also the rights of employees who are harmed even though the actual unwanted sexual behavior was not directed at them.

CHAPTER • TWO

Background And Development Of Sexual Harassment As A Legal Claim

Laws come from two places: statutes enacted by legislatures (state and federal) and decisions made by courts. In addition, the United States has a constitution which is considered "the supreme law of the land." The constitution protects individual rights by making sure that statutes and court decisions are fair. In effect, a statute or court decision is considered fair if it does not violate the constitution.

In 1964 Congress (the federal legislature) passed the Civil Rights Act in a major effort to prohibit discrimination on the basis of race, color, religion, national origin or sex. The Civil Rights Act operates in many arenas, but the part that relates to sexual harassment is known as "Title VII" which forbids discrimination in employment on the basis of race, sex, etc. (Title IX is also important because it makes discrimination in education illegal for the same reasons.) [The only exception to Title VII occurs if an employer must make an employment decision on the basis of one of these factors, e.g., sex because it is a necessary qualification for the job. This is known as a "business necessity" or "bona fide occupational qualification" and really has no connection to sexual harassment.]

In 1977 a federal court ruled that sexual harassment is a form of discrimination on the basis of sex. Since that case involved an employment situation, the court held that sexual harassment violates Title VII. The court maintained that if a plaintiff can show that she suffered sexual harassment, the law must provide a remedy.

A remedy is a means of correcting a bad condition and making it right or compensating a victim for the difficulty she has suffered. The purpose of this chapter is to provide an understanding of the law and explain why it is what it is. Chapter 4 will address the procedures, both practical and legal, for pursuing the available remedies.

The Structure Behind The Law: Sorting Out What To Do

In addition to Title VII, Congress created the Equal Employment Opportunity Commission (EEOC) for the specific purpose of enforcing Title VII and other Acts dealing with the right to equal opportunity in employment. The EEOC is a federal agency. Its specific task is to enforce federal law. It has four major statutory functions: investigating claims and correcting the situation if possible, enforcing Title VII, issuing official guidelines to interpret Title VII, and enforcing the law. The EEOC specifically goes after federal employers but also has jurisdiction over some city, state or private employers. It also has the ultimate power to determine whether you can sue in federal court under Title VII because federal law requires you to file first with the EEOC before going to court.

In 1986 the United States Supreme Court heard the first major case addressing sexual harassment in employment. In *Meritor Savings Bank, FSB v. Vinson,* the Court declared that no court or legislature could create a law that denies that sexual harassment is against the law. In so ruling, it upheld the EEOC guidelines forbidding sexual harassment in the workplace.

So You Think You Have A Complaint: What You Should Know

Meritor Savings Bank and the EEOC guidelines recognize two types of sexual harassment: *quid pro quo* ("tit for tat") harassment in which the victim is asked for some form of sexual favors (as discussed in Chapter 1) in exchange for some job-related benefit (e.g., a promotion); and "poisoned" or hostile workplace harassment, in which the victim has been forced to put up with conduct of a sexual nature that makes the work environment uncomfortable (e.g., dirty jokes or pin-ups on the walls). Both types of harassment are now illegal and, if proven, can require the employer to correct the situation and perhaps pay money to a victim.

The first successful sexual harassment case was brought in 1977 in the District of Columbia. It was the *quid pro quo* type. In that case a male supervisor retaliated against a female employee who declined his sexual advances. The court held that "retaliation" constitutes sexual discrimination within the meaning of Title VII. Such retaliatory actions can range from outright firing, to refusal to grant an otherwise deserved promotion, to forcing the harassed employee into quitting. The law calls this last situation "constructive firing" and, in addition to the remedies under Title VII, in many states the employee may also be able to receive unemployment or workers' compensation benefits. The *quid pro quo* sexual harassment case is the easier case for the law to address because the "harm" complained of — loss of job or denial of job-related benefit — is easier to remedy. In short, the law can put a price on the victim's harm. By comparison, it is more difficult to put a price on a "hostile work environment," which a victim puts up with for a long period of time.

There have also been situations in which an employee is discriminated against because a relative refuses to be "harassed" — to grant sexual favors to a supervisor. For example, if the boss attempts to harass Jack's wife and she declines his advances, only to have the boss fire Jack, he, too, may have a complaint of *quid pro quo* sexual harassment under Title VII. The bottom line is whether or not a job or job-related benefit was conditioned on sexual favors.

The "hostile work environment" type of sexual harassment is newer and more difficult to identify and to remedy. Courts are asked to remedy not only a firing or a lost promotion but also the "purely psychological aspects of the workplace environment." The Supreme Court reasoned in *Meritor* that any conduct which is sexual in nature and severe enough to psychologically upset an employee is unlawful sex discrimination under Title VII. In order to win under a "hostile work environment" type of sexual harassment claim, the employee must be able to show that the harassment has interfered with her ability to work or has significantly affected her psychological well-being. She must also show that the harassment would have a similar effect on any "reasonable" person of the same gender.

This standard is important because a recent case held that what constitutes sexual harassment should be looked at from the victim's perspective. That the conduct is common does not matter. Also irrelevant is the fact that the average man might not be bothered by it. The court noted that "conduct that many men consider unobjectionable may offend many women . . . [And while] we realize that there is a broad range of viewpoints among women as a group . . . we believe that many women share common concerns which men do not necessarily share." Other courts are also beginning to adopt the position that the severity of harassing conduct should be determined from the victim's point of view.

Even given this new standard, victims of sexual harassment will still have to prove that the conduct happened over and over again. In other words, there was a pattern of repeated harassment. A single instance will rarely qualify. Further, victims of sexual harassment must prove that the conduct was unwelcomed, was sexual in nature and that the employer knew or should have known of the harassment. Appearing to "go along with" the harassment or appearing to put up with it is not necessarily the same thing as "welcoming" it and such a situation may still qualify.

Under the law, men as well as women may bring complaints of sexual harassment. After all, sexual harassment is unlawful discrimination on the basis of gender, and gender means gender, plain and simple. In fact, each year several hundred men file charges with the EEOC. As a practical matter, however, statistics have shown that the overwhelming majority of sexual harassment victims are women. Some statistics also show that at least 50 percent of all working women have reported experiencing some form of sexual harassment. In addition, there is nothing in the law which requires that the harasser and the victim be of different sexes. Any type of sexual pressure on the job which the victim feels has an adverse impact on his or her work could be considered sexual harassment. Statistics also show that in many of the cases that men bring for sexual harassment, the harasser was also a man. Cases have also been brought against women by other women.

Some Related Legal Issues

Sexual Harassment And Date Rape

Date rape, like sexual harassment, has only recently been brought out into the open as a "social" occurrence to which women are subjected. Society as a whole has been unwilling to accept the idea that rape could be committed by someone with whom the victim was friendly or acquainted and with whom she shared a dating relationship.

The highly publicized rape cases of William Kennedy Smith and Mike Tyson have heightened the awareness of "date rape." Criminal laws in all states define "rape" as nonconsensual sexual intercourse. The lack of consent on the part of the victim refers to the present circumstances and not the prior relationship (or lack of it) between the parties. Needless to say, just as women are the principal victims of sexual harassment, so also are women the principal victims of date rape.

It may appear, at first, that date rape (nonconsensual sexual intercourse initiated in a social context) is one issue and sexual harassment (unwelcome sexual coercion in the workplace context) is another. So why discuss date rape in a book about surviving sexual harassment in the workplace? In reality the two issues are not that separate. A person's workplace has been called the second most important environment in a person's life next to the family. For many people their work is *the* most important relationship in their lives. This has become true for increasing numbers of women, especially as they try to "move up the corporate ladder." Take two examples:

- Molly is a young, rising, middle-level manager in a large national corporation. Her work requires her and other employees to travel to business meetings in distant cities. She is one of the few women at this level, and most of her fellow managers are men. One evening after a particularly long business meeting one of the senior managers asked her to accompany him back to his room in the hotel in order to get some reports and discuss what had occurred at the meeting. Their prior relationship had been close and friendly. They had often had meals together, but they had never gone beyond the bounds of professionalism.

    When they went to the hotel room, her male co-worker assaulted her. She resisted vigorously. Her clothing was torn, and she received some bruises. He broke off the attack just short of actual penetration, stating that he had had his eye on her for some time and had assumed she "wanted it."

    When they met the next day, her attacker told her that if she tried to tell anyone in the company about what occurred, no one would believe her. He even went as far as threatening her safety if she tried to press charges. She stayed with the company for two more years, but ultimately left because of the stress she felt in continuing to work with her attacker.

To this day, she continues to feel the aftershocks of that night. She has never spoken of the assault to anyone outside of her closest circle of friends and family.

- Harriet is a senior executive secretary working in a multi-national corporation overseas. She has been with her boss for a number of years and with the company even longer. As he has risen, so has she. As is frequently the case in foreign countries, all the Americans tend to live in a compound within the city, just within a short distance of each other. Everyone knows everyone else, and socializing within the American community is a regular occurrence. As Harriet is single, she lives alone in an apartment about five minutes by car from where her boss lives with his family. It is not uncommon for her boss to stop by with work for her. Occasionally, he has simply stopped by for a casual chat and a drink before going on home. Several times her boss has given her a ride home from the office.

  On one occasion, however, after they came in the apartment, her boss slammed the door, threw her to the floor and raped her. Despite the attack, Harriet managed to make it to work the next day. Her boss apologized but also told her that if she ever spoke of the incident, she would ruin both their careers.

  She did go to an individual higher up in the organization whom she trusted but was told that there was really nothing he could do. He offered to transfer her to another office into a position equal to the one she occupied. She accepted the offer even though she would have preferred to stay where she was in a city with which she had become familiar. No charges were ever brought.

Sexual harassment or date rape? There is no "bright line" between the two in situations where the workplace and the social contexts become blended. Certainly, the atmosphere in the workplace for the victim in such situations becomes poisoned, but the facts may or may not fit either the classic *quid pro quo* or "hostile work environment" scenarios that Title VII has been used to remedy. Some courts have even ruled that a sexual assault that occurs outside the workplace, even if committed by a co-worker, is outside the type of harm that Title VII was intended to redress because the actual assault occurred in a non-work situation. Sexual assault, these courts reason, is a crime and should be handled by the criminal legal system. Title VII is a *civil* rights law, not part of federal criminal law. Additionally, as there are virtually never any witnesses to the assault, accusations can come down to a "she said/he said" type of situation. If the victim does press criminal charges, she will have to prove "beyond a reasonable doubt" that an assault did take place. This can be a very tough hurdle to get over — doubly so because not only did the individuals involved demonstrate previously cordial relations, but also because in many cases the victim sees no choice but to stay on the job as long as she can "take it." Furthermore, should the victim be fired as a result of bringing charges, she may well subject herself to accusations of reacting as a "spurned woman," delusional and, therefore, a trouble-maker. Nevertheless, Title VII does recognize and cover complaints of "retaliatory discharge." Here, the victim must demonstrate that she was fired because she brought the complaint, provided, however, that what she suffered was also employment-related sexual harassment and that she was discharged specifically because she brought the charge.

The victim may or may not have a remedy under state law, but this depends on many variables. Obviously, if her alleged attacker has been involved in other incidents with other female co-workers, she may have a genuine chance of successfully bringing a charge of negligent supervision against the higher ups in the organization and she can show that they knew or should have known that the male co-worker involved had engaged in such behavior in the past. This is also providing that the law of her state allows her to bring such a complaint since not all states recognize a complaint based on negligent supervision.

On the other hand, if her attacker *is* the higher up she could be stopped right there whether or not the state recognizes such a complaint. Other possible bases for bringing a civil complaint (which later chapters discuss in detail) are civil (as opposed to criminal) battery and intentional infliction of emotional distress. Successful cases have been brought under both these theories.

As a general rule of thumb, the more outrageous the conduct, the greater the chance of bringing a successful case.

Sexual Harassment By Proxy

In Chapter 1 we discussed the possibility of "outside" parties bringing a complaint for employment discrimination because they were denied employment-related benefits in favor of a fellow employee who was granted these benefits because she gave in to requests for sexual favors from the person in a position to grant these benefits. The law calls this type of complaint a "third party" complaint because these individuals were parties who were outside the immediate employee/employer sexual favor situation but still suffered harm as a direct result of it. The prohibited behavior occurs between A and B, but because of it, C, D and E also suffer harm. C, D and E can sue A. B also can sue A. C, D and E have all suffered discrimination in employment because of gender — A's favoritism to B because of B's acquiescence to A's requests, and B has an employment discrimination claim (here, *quid pro quo* sexual harassment) against A because her employment benefits were conditioned on her granting him sexual favors.

Quid pro quo sexual harassment can include yet another type of "third party" compaint: one in which the party directly "hit on" and the ultimate "target" may both have a cause of action based on sexual harassment. For example:

- Bernice has worked for some time in the company where Walter is a supervisor responsible for hiring and firing. Her daughter, Marjorie, has just graduated from college and is well-qualified for a position that has just opened up in the company. Marjorie applies for the job. When Walter learns of Marjorie's application, he tells Bernice that he will definitely make sure that Marjorie is hired for the position — providing that Bernice can convince Marjorie that there are certain other "application requirements" which will be necessary before Marjorie gets the job. Walter continues to press Bernice about the "job requirements" and keeps the job open pending their reply. Both women refuse Walter's "proposal." Not only is Marjorie's application refused, but Bernice is also ultimately "let go."

- Joe and his wife, Janine, both work for a large company on an assembly line. Joe's position is slightly senior to his wife's because of his longer employment there. Janine, however, has been in her position for a long enough period that she also has seniority over a number of other employees of both sexes. At the same time, however, there are individuals on the line who have seniority equal to both Joe and Janine. Matt is a supervisor on the line. One day, Matt comes to Joe and informs him that he has been ordered to lay off several people on the line because of reduced business. He informs Joe that both he and Janine are on the list along with several others, but that he can "see to it" that neither Joe nor his wife is laid off, providing that Janine can demonstrate that the couple has "something extra" that will convince Matt that neither of them should be laid off.

Here, Joe has an employment discrimination complaint against Matt and his superiors based on gender — Janine's. In addition, she has an employment discrimination complaint on the same basis, plus an additional complaint based on *quid pro quo* sexual harassment: the condition of their continued employment based on her willingness to confer sexual favors on Matt.

In addition, the other individuals on the list may also have an employment discrimination complaint against Matt and the company if they can show that the company "knew or should have known" of such practices. Obviously the lay-off itself is not the "impermissible practice" nor is the condition of the decision on whom to lay off according to seniority. What is illegal is conditioning the decision on whom to lay off on factors not related to the job itself, e.g., seniority or expertise in doing the job.

One final note here: Joe, Janine and their coworkers may be members of a union. If so, they will all be required to work according to their union's contract grievance procedures in their collective bargaining agreement with the company. The possible further complications of this and the background behind it are beyond the scope of this handbook, however. Suffice it to say that if you work for a union, national labor policy requires you to look to your union first.

Worker's Compensation Meets Sexual Harassment

Earlier in this chapter we mentioned that victims of sexual harassment may now be eligible for worker's compensation benefits. In Chapter 1 we also discussed the psychological harm that victims of sexual harassment can and do suffer. Up until recently, state and federal courts were not willing to consider compensating victims of sexual harassment for anything but physical injuries, but this is changing.

Worker's or Workmen's Compensation laws were passed in this country during the first half of this century. The policy behind them was to provide every worker injured on the job with some sort of medical coverage for these injuries as well as living expenses during any necessary period of convalescence. "Medical expenses" include hospitalization, if necessary, plus doctor's bills, medicine and "out-patient" treatment, such as physical therapy. "Convalescence" means that period of time that you need to get well and are not able to go back to work, either to the job you were doing when you were hurt or to a job with roughly similar qualifications and/or pay.

Prior to the passage of these laws, if you were injured on the job, the only thing you could do to try to get compensation for your injuries was to sue the employer. Worker's compensation laws not only make this unnecessary, they "stand in the place" of this right to sue your employer. In effect, the system is a trade-off. You cannot sue your employer for on-the-job injuries specifically because you are covered by worker's compensation. Under the old system you might have received more, but — more typically — you would have received much less or even nothing at all.

Federal law requires that each state have some sort of worker's compensation system in place. Apart from some rough guidelines and the general limitation of the United States Constitution and federal labor laws, however, each state administers its own system and can set maximum levels of compensation both for medical expenses and convalescence. State boards administer their state's system and regularly review the injured person's continued eligibility to receive benefits. In short, they decide when you are well enough to go back to work. If you (and your doctor) disagree, you can argue with them, i.e., appeal their decision.

There are many lawyers who specialize in helping you to present your case, and worker's compensation laws generally cover any legal expenses that you might incur in presenting your appeal to your worker's compensation board's decision to terminate benefits. There is also a federal worker's compensation law ("Federal Employees' Compensation Act") which covers federal workers and individuals who work in Washington, D.C.

When worker's compensation systems were first put in place, the type of injuries that the lawmakers had in mind were the "obvious" ones: broken limbs, gashed heads or loss of vision and hearing. Debilitating psychological injuries were not explicitly considered by the people who wrote these laws. These were not explicitly excluded either, however. When disputes over denial of benefits and the proper extent of coverage under worker's compensation laws reached the courts, they, too, tended to look to the traditional definition of "injury." Work-related "shell shock," while unfortunate, was ruled as ineligible for coverage under worker's compensation. What this meant for victims of sexual harassment was that they were out of luck as far as getting any financial help under worker's compensation to cover the costs of treating their problems, both psychological and physical.

As the social climate toward the acceptability of sexual harassment is changing, so too are state courts' willingness to expand the definition of "work-related injury" to include any sort of injury suffered in the workplace. Not every state's courts are equally generous, but the trend is to require that compensation be extended to any "significant" injury that the victim can show was the direct result of the work environment. In short, if the victim of sexual harassment can show that the harassment she suffered so "unhinged" her that she now requires professional (psychiatric or psychological) help to deal with her job, she may well be able to get this help covered under her state's worker's compensation system. Any physical side effects of the harassment, such as stomach disorders, which may require hospitalization, may also be covered if the victim (and her doctor) can show that but for the harassment that the victim suffered she would not have become sick.

Sexual Harassment And Unemployment Compensation

Like Worker's Compensation, Unemployment Compensation is state administered. Unlike Worker's Compensation, however, it is the federal government that sets limits on how long unemployment benefits can be paid to people out of work. It is a flat period whose maximum length is determined by how long Congress is willing to extend it. The states decide who meets eligibility requirements and set standards for meeting those requirements. As a general rule, if you are fired or laid off, you are eligible to apply for unemployment, but if you leave your job "voluntarily," you will not be eligible for unemployment. What this used to mean for victims of sexual harassment was that if they left their jobs only because they saw no other way to escape the harassment, they were still deemed to have left their jobs voluntarily. Because they left their jobs "voluntarily," they were ineligible for unemployment.

Here, again, application of the law is changing. This is where the legal concepts of "constructive firing" or "constructive termination" become applicable. In the law, the term "constructive" is used as a sort of shorthand to say "It is as good as if . . ." or "So close to such and such that it might as well be . . ." Here, "constructive firing or termination" means that the treatment suffered by the victim was so bad for her that it is "just as if" she were actually fired. She was made to quit because of the harassment; therefore, the law will treat her as if she had actually been fired. Since the law, under these circumstances, will treat the victim of sexual harassment as if she had actually been fired, she will be eligible to receive unemployment benefits on the same terms as anyone else who was fired or laid off.

Some Final Words On "Sexual" Harassment

Readers of this handbook may have noted that while mention has been made of situations where the harasser and the person harassed need not be of different genders to have a claim of sexual harassment, no mention has been made of the harassment that members of the gay and lesbian community daily endure on their jobs because of their sexual orientation. This is not a reflection on the authors' sense of the gravity of this problem. It is a very serious problem for which there is still no adequate remedy under civil rights or employment law. Unfortunately, neither Title VII nor its state versions were intended to bring sexual orientation within its scope of protection. Simply put, discrimination because of sexual orientation is not regarded by the law as the same thing as discrimination because of gender.

Several states do have laws which prohibit discrimination against an individual because of sexual orientation, but these laws are not "Title VII-type" laws. To date, no one has successfully sued under Title VII — in either the state or federal courts — because of employment discrimination due to sexual orientation. The time may come when the coverage of Title VII will change to include sexual orientation among its protected categories but that time is still in the future. Those who suffer harassment because of their sexual orientation must look either to their states' tort laws which are dealt with in greater detail in Chapter 4 or any specialized state gay anti-discrimination laws to seek redress for the wrongs that they suffer.

CASE HISTORY: Lorene

I have wanted to be a doctor since I was about nine years old. My pediatrician was such a kind and dignified person and always seemed to know how to make me feel better. When you know what career you want to pursue, you can start working on it early. I started preparing to become a doctor in the third grade.

At seventeen I was accepted to a terrific Ivy League college. I knew how important those four years would be. I was very focused and did well — until I encountered Organic Chemistry. This was a very important pre-med subject and I was having a lot of trouble with it. The labs were particularly difficult for me and I began to put in extra hours which usually occurred in the evening after dinner. One night when I was working late, my professor came into the lab and expressed surprise at finding me there.

Let me tell you a little about my professor, Dr. P. He was about forty years old. He wore glasses, was beginning to lose his hair, but seemed in pretty good physical shape. He had been at the college forever and somewhere along the way had been married and divorced. You have to understand that we are talking about a small community. People tend to know a lot about each other and rumors are always flying around.

The rumor about Dr. P. was that his marriage broke up when his wife discovered that he was having an affair with one of his students. There were other rumors about Dr. P. and some of his students but the fact was that he was a tenured professor and as far as anyone knew, he had never had any problems with his bosses, the college administration. As far as I was concerned, he always seemed to have a pleasant, mild manner, seemed devoted to teaching and research, and seemed like the kind of teacher you would want to be your mentor and help you through.

When Dr. P. came into the lab that night, I could not have been more pleased to see anybody. I had been working on a particularly difficult experiment and I could not get it right. I was really getting frustrated. It was pretty obvious, too, and Dr. P. commented that I looked upset and wondered what the matter was.

Well, all I needed was a friendly word and I began to tell him my life story. I told him I was very upset because I was having so much trouble with his course. I was worried because it was an important pre-med requirement. I had wanted to be a doctor since I was nine and I would not be able to get into medical school, etc., etc. He let me go on and seemed very sympathetic. When I finished ranting, he told me not to worry, he personally would help me and getting a good grade would not be a problem. He showed me what I was doing incorrectly with the experiment I was working on and I began to relax as a sense of relief swept over me.

Dr. P. began meeting me at the lab after dinner. At first he was very patient and helpful. Within a week I began getting funny feelings. As I was working the experiment, Dr. P. would come over and stand behind me, as though he was watching me work but his breathing would feel very close and would get faster. Then he would seem to brush up against me. I felt scared and confused and did not know what to do, so I did nothing. I sort of froze inside while I pretended to go about my work. But I was losing my ability to concentrate and made mistakes. That gave him more reason to "closely supervise" my work until one night he actually leaned his body against mine from behind, wrapped his arms around me, and began to touch my breasts. I thought I would die. I broke his embrace, moved away from him and began to shake and stammer. I said I did not know why he was doing this and that I wanted him to stop. I told him that I wanted his help but I did not want this.

My helpful Ivy League professor looked at me with the kind of smile on his face that I had only seen before in movies. He said that he found me very attractive and that he could think of nothing but me since he first ran into me that night in the lab. He said he wanted to help and guide me and that he intended our relationship to "deepen" and become very intimate. He said that he would see me in class the next day and meet me in the lab that evening. He said I should come prepared to "learn about life" and that he would make an "exceptional" teacher.

I went home very upset. I was nervous, depressed and also very angry. I did not know what to do or who to talk to. I cried a lot. I did not want to go to class the next day, but I knew I could not just drop out. I decided to write Dr. P. a letter and hand it to him at the end of class.

I did just that. I hoped that when he read the letter, he would realize that I admired him but did not feel romantic toward him and wanted him to please stop coming on to me. I told him he was upsetting me and interfering with my studies.

That night as I struggled to concentrate and stay focused, Dr. P. came into the lab. He took my hand, put his arm around me and said that I was naive and did not understand what I needed to do to be successful. He told me that he could make sure that I got an "A" in the course, as well as a strong recommendation for med school and that he could influence other faculty toward me. If becoming a doctor was that important to me, then I should be more than willing to "go along with the program." As he bent his head to kiss me, I broke away and ran out of the lab. I was too shaken up to go back to my room so I went to the college infirmary. The nurse on duty quieted me down and made arrangements for me to see a counselor the next day.

The counselor was very understanding and listened sympathetically to my story. I felt that this was not the first time she had heard it. She explained to me what I could do. She said I could file a formal complaint with the president's office. There would then be a hearing. It would probably take the rest of the academic year to complete, and I must recognize that it was Dr. P.'s word against mine. The more acceptable alternative was the most practical one — drop the course. That's the one I chose and stayed as far away from the chemistry department as possible.

What Happened?

Lorene realized that if she wanted to pursue her dream of medical school, she would have to take organic chemistry and the other required chemistry courses. That was not easily done without encountering Dr. P. again. She decided to complete the semester and transfer what credits she could salvage to her local state university. There she completed her studies successfully and uneventfully. She is presently in her third year of medical school and planning to become a psychiatrist.

Discussion

Lorene's case is presented as an example of the type of sexual harassment that occurs in educational institutions. Even though school is not a workplace, the court in *Alexander vs. Yale* (1977) decided that sexual harassment constitutes a form of sex discrimination that denies equal access to educational opportunities. Lorene's story is one of *quid pro quo* harassment within an educational setting. It is a typical story of an ambitious female student being coerced into a sexual relationship by a male faculty member who has the power to affect a student's grades and even the student's future education and/or career. The key elements in Lorene's case are: Dr. P's offer to help Lorene in exchange for her sexual favors; his leering, embracing and fondling Lorene against her wishes; his refusal to stop the unwanted behavior when asked to by Lorene; and his threat to affect the attitudes of other faculty toward Lorene, thus ultimately affecting her graduate education and career. Despite the availability of a grievance mechanism, Lorene chose a more immediate, practical solution by dropping Dr. P's course and, at the earliest opportunity, changing colleges. Lorene chose not to pursue the legal remedies available to her, even though her situation clearly had recourse available.

CHAPTER • THREE

Practical, Informal And Formal Complaint Procedures And Remedies

The authors writing this handbook have made the assumption that someone interested in the topic of sexual harassment has either been victimized, knows someone who has or is worried that it could happen to her. This chapter will address ways to deal with sexual harassment and remedies currently available, including those in the 1991 Amendment to the Civil Rights Act. Before discussing complaint procedures and remedies, this section will suggest some ideas which could either reduce the occurrence of sexual harassment or address it when the danger signs first appear.

Psychologists have been studying various aspects of sexual harassment for about ten years. Much of their research has focused on male-female differences in the perception of male-female interaction. Some of these studies have shown that when women at work or school strive to create a pleasant, warm and friendly social environment, male colleagues often see this behavior as seductive and a sign of sexual interest and availability. Men are thus more likely to put the responsibility for a sexual harassment incident onto the female victim, who is seen as "asking for it." In addition, research has shown that male managers also differ from females in that they view what many women will experience as sexual harassment as normal male behavior and no "big deal," i.e., not a problem. These findings suggest that male-female differences, when not understood, can lead to unintended consequences.

This is particularly true in today's world where the workplace is, for many people, a major part of their social environment. It is not only the place to work and make a living, but also where social and romantic contacts can be made. While this is not likely to change, people should recognize that the workplace is for work and that how people conduct themselves in that workplace should be related to getting the job done. This calls for discretion in choosing how to dress, in making or allowing physical contact, in offering non-work performance related comments or compliments, and in discussing intimate personal or sexual matters.

Men and women tend to interpret these comments differently so that it is important to conduct yourself at work or school in such a way as to minimize the possibility that the behavior will be misinterpreted and an incident will occur. Unfortunately, there are too many instances when these preventative steps have not worked. A victim may be exposed to repeated requests for dates, unnecessary, unwelcome and offensive touching, sharing, being followed around the workplace or sexual innuendoes and obscene comments and gestures.

What To Do: STOP!

If the harassment has not escalated to the point that going to work is like being trapped in a nightmare nor does the victim feel physically threatened and on the emotional "edge," she should try to get the harasser to stop before proceeding to make any formal or informal complaints. Victims of sexual harassment choosing this option should know that there are certain things that they can do.

Tell the harasser in no uncertain terms that his behavior is *not* welcome and should stop immediately. Additionally, harassment victims may choose to make their statements in writing as well as verbally, keeping a copy for their own personal file. They should also tell people outside of work, such as family, friends and even their doctor, about what is going on and how they are trying to deal with it. A written journal of the harassing events should be kept as well as any efforts the victim has made to try to stop the unwanted behavior.

Personal journals may include such information as: the type of unwanted behavior (i.e., verbal, physical or both), how frequently it occurs, how it is hostile and offensive, who the harasser is (i.e., co-worker, supervisor or boss) and if other people participated in the harassment.

Also remember, what matters is how the *victim* feels or perceives these incidents, not how others might perceive them. In other words, it is important that the *victim*, personally, is bothered by the incidents, not that others might not be bothered. If possible, victims should share their experiences with co-workers to see whether they also have had the same problem with the same person. If there is a pattern to the harasser's behavior, it may suggest how he will interpret and deal with the victim's request to stop this behavior. If he does not stop, any evidence establishing that it is a pattern will be helpful to the victim's case should she ultimately decide to file a complaint.

One of the most important things to remember is that the sexual harassment is often more an expression of a perpetrator's need to exercise power and control than sexual desire. In fact, in cases in which the harassment occurs as a result of an honest misinterpretation or misperception and is primarily sexually driven, not power driven, telling the perpetrator to stop will clear up the misperceptions. He may try to save face in some way, but he will stop his unwanted behavior. If the perpetrator is power driven, however, he is likely to persist as long as his victim remains passive, frightened and compliant. The perpetrator may threaten his victim with loss of a promotion, special benefits or the job itself and even public embarrassment.

Facing one's fear and expressing outrage are the most effective ways to stop the controlling and threatening behavior.

What Else To Do: File An Informal Complaint

If asking or even demanding that the unwanted sexually harassing behavior stop does not lead to a satisfactory result, the harassment victim may want to file either an informal complaint or a formal grievance. While having made an initial protest may be helpful to the victim's case, it is not an absolutely necessary step to take in order to file a formal grievance. In fact, even if the victim was initially reluctant to complain, she may still file an informal complaint or a formal grievance. It is important to understand the differences between informal and formal procedures so that an intelligent choice can be made. Each has its advantages and drawbacks, and each person must decide which approach is most suitable to her needs and circumstances.

The Informal Complaint

The goal of filing an informal complaint is to solve the problem of being sexually harassed and to get it to stop, rather than to put the perpetrator on trial. The choice of the informal procedure is best if both parties come to see that a problem exists, want it solved and believe that they can reach an agreement that is mutually satisfactory. The goal is to end the harassment as perceived by the victim. It is *not* to judge or punish the accused perpetrator.

The major concern is not on what happened in the past, but rather on what will occur between the parties in the future. There are, typically, no set procedures setting forth how this will occur. There are no formal hearing or review boards, and lawyers need not be involved — although each party may be represented by an advocate or counsel. Informal efforts are made to negotiate a satisfactory agreement between the parties, such as having an unbiased person mediate the resolution of the complaint. The procedure is completed when the victim feels satisfied that the sexual harassment will be or has stopped. Compliance with the agreement is voluntary.

The Formal Grievance

Unlike informal procedures, formal grievance procedures have an identifiable structure and follow a specified course. A formal grievance usually requires filing a written complaint with an official group such as a hearing board. This official group investigates the charges to determine the guilt or innocence of the accused harasser. These hearings *are* like a trial; lawyers often represent each party and the process ends when the hearing board determines which party will prevail. Depending on the situation, if there is a finding of guilt, punishment will be decided by the appropriate officer of the company or institution. Compliance with the hearing results are mandatory, *not* voluntary. They can be appealed to the next higher authority.

An informal complaint procedure is usually chosen when the person filing the complaint wants to reestablish a harmonious relationship between the parties. It is useful in resolving conflict but is not for the purpose of determining how justice would best be served. There are no remedies involved other than restoring peace within the environment that the victim and perpetrator share.

The formal grievance process is a legal procedure directed by federal and state laws and regulations and provides for specific remedies governed by these laws.

Bringing A Formal Complaint: Jumping Through The Hoops

What To Do First And Why

If attempts at informal face-to-face resolution of the sexual harassment have not met with success, victims should next consider pursuing their complaints through more formal procedures. Victims of sexual harassment should keep in mind that the law views the behavior complained of from their point of view plus what is often referred to as a "totality of the circumstances." The sexual harassment victim has already complained to the harasser that such speech, touching and/or other mannerisms are not appreciated; in a word, "unwelcomed." Management refused to stop the complained-of behavior.

What the victim does next depends on whether she is still in her job or whether she has already left or been fired. In both cases, however, it will definitely be of help, but not absolutely necessary, if the victim has kept a record of the incidents and has discussed what she has been experiencing with other people, especially friendly co-workers. They may later serve as corroborating witnesses. Proof of a pattern of abusive behavior will be very important to an harassment victim's case, although one especially violent incident, such as a rape, is sufficient.

If she is still at her job, and the company the two people work for has an established grievance procedure to deal with workplace complaints, the law encourages, but does not require, victims of harassment to use this procedure. If the victim is still on the job, there may be good reasons to choose to go through the in-house grievance procedure.

For example, even if using these procedures does not solve the problem, the victim may have at least strengthened her case for a lawsuit. It is also important to know that if one is fired as a result of having made a complaint, the firing is unlawful under Title VII. Employees may not be fired for exercising their constitutionally protected rights under this law.

Beginning The Legal Process

Victims of sexual harassment should consider bringing a lawsuit if they have not reached a satisfactory solution and still believe that their legal rights have been violated. Most, but not all, people who bring lawsuits hire an attorney to represent them. One reason that attorneys are helpful, particularly in the beginning stages of this type of lawsuit, is that the procedures for getting into court are complicated, and the time frame for moving along this type of case may be very short such as 60 or 90 days. There are also a number of different ways of approaching the problem legally that might be useful in these cases. Both the procedure and the legal bases for this type of claim will be outlined here. However, this is intended as an overview and not a "how-to" manual for people who choose to represent themselves instead of being represented by an attorney.

Victims of harassment are often deterred from pursuing their claims because of the cost of legal services. One way of avoiding exorbitant out-of-pocket costs is "contingent fee" arrangements, which many lawyers will accept instead of hourly charges. Under such an agreement, the lawyer does not charge the person bringing the complaint (the "plaintiff") but instead takes a percentage of her ultimate award, if and when it is recovered. If the person bringing the complaint loses, she pays no legal fee except for some court and other costs associated with the suit. The question of whether a case will be taken by a lawyer on a contingent fee basis may depend on the lawyer's willingness to make such an arrangement and the nature of the case. A great advantage of a Title VII-type of action is that the statute does allow for court costs, should it come to that, and attorney's fees, if any. Under the 1991 Amendment to the Civil Rights Act recently signed by President Bush, fees associated with calling in expert witnesses are also covered by Title VII.

Some plaintiffs attempt to represent themselves and bring their own cases through court. However, because of the complicated procedures outlined below, doing it oneself incurs the substantial risk that a procedure will not be completed properly. There are also additional risks to trying to litigate on one's own and while it is possible to do, it is probably wiser to engage an experienced attorney.

The following pages present a rough sketch and are offered with the warning that each state makes its own rules, and no two are identical. You need to know the rules of your own state.

Filing The Complaint

Once any in-house grievance procedures have been exhausted, the next place to go is the agency responsible for enforcing the state's antidiscrimination laws. The federal EEOC cannot look at any complaint before the state agency has had a particular case for at least 60 calendar days.

There are three general exceptions to this rule:

1. If the victim is or was working for a federal agency to begin with,
2. If the victim is or was employed in the District of Columbia,
3. If the state where the harassment occurred has no such agency.

Most, but not all, states do have some sort of agency responsible for enforcing discrimination laws. Each state has a local federal EEOC office that should be able to answer questions on this score. A complete list of the addresses of each federal EEOC office is at the end of this book.

It is also important to point out that many companies are too small to be subject to Title VII's coverage, employing fewer than 15 people. Victims of sexual harassment may then choose to pursue their rights according to other state laws. Many states have statutes or law stemming from court decisions which allow suit for such things as "intentional infliction of emotional distress," "wrongful termination" and others which may apply to the victim's particular case. Sexual harassment victims may also have the option of claiming these wrongs in addition to any Title VII employment discrimination complaints.

Assuming that one's company does not fall within any of the exceptions listed above and is large enough to fall within Title VII's coverage, the next step is to file a claim with the appropriate state agency as required by federal law. As previously stated, the EEOC will not review any complaint unless the state agency has had it for at least 60 calendar days. *Time is of the essence.* The law cannot grant a remedy to plaintiffs if they wait too long to file their complaint. In employment discrimination complaints, this time is particularly short — a mere matter of months from the time the complained-of behavior last occurred. Therefore, anyone who believes that she has been the victim of sexual harassment and feels that her work has suffered should file sooner rather than later.

In With The EEOC: What Next?

Once the EEOC gets a complaint, it has ten days to notify the employer that a charge of employment discrimination has been filed against it, and then to conduct an investigation to determine if there is reasonable cause to believe that the charge is true. As a practical matter, EEOC action is now almost never that swift. Once the investigation is finished, however, the EEOC can take one of two courses: It can find "reasonable cause" or it can find "no reasonable cause" that unlawful employment discrimination has occurred.

A finding of "reasonable cause" means not only that the EEOC will take the case, but also that *only* the EEOC can proceed on the victim's behalf. The harassment victim can no longer sue on her own.

The first thing that the EEOC is required to do under Title VII is attempt a reconciliation between the alleged victim and her employer. If this does not work, the agency may bring a civil suit against the defendant-employer in federal district court. However, if the EEOC does not sue within about six months from the filing of the charge, the harassment victim (plaintiff) may request a "right-to-sue" letter. The letter allows the plaintiff three months or 90 days in which to file suit on their own in federal district court.

One can also choose to allow the EEOC to carry the process through to its conclusion and then bring suit within 90 days of that point. If the EEOC finds "no reasonable cause," it will dismiss the charge and notify the individual who brought the charge of the dismissal. This does not necessarily mean that there is no case. Victims of sexual harassment may still sue on their own behalf in federal district court. This may obviously be confusing and demonstrates the wisdom of hiring a lawyer.

The requirements for filing were designed with the layperson in mind. The EEOC and most state antidiscrimination agencies use what is frequently called an "Intake Questionnaire." Several federal courts have already ruled that this form could constitute a valid complaint, even though it is unsigned and unverified and the actual formal complaint is not completed until later. As a practical matter, the only requirement seems to be that the complaint be in writing and identify the parties and the conduct or practices which resulted in the complaint. According to the federal regulation on the subject:

> "A charge is sufficient when the Commission (the EEOC) receives from the complainant a written statement sufficiently precise to identify the parties and to describe generally the action or practice complained of."

State regulations covering the filing of an employment discrimination charge with their antidiscrimination agencies generally follow similar rules.

Whom To Sue And Why

The party against which suit in a Title VII complaint should be brought is the victim's employer. This may be an individual or it may be a whole company. It is the employer who is liable for harm suffered in the employer's workplace. If one's employer is the harasser, the question of who is ultimately responsible is simple. Only one individual is involved. However, even if the employer is a large company, it may still be held responsible for the acts of its employees carried out within the scope of their employment. Courts are now fairly uniform in their rulings that in sexual harassment cases in which the victim's supervisor is the harasser, the company may be held responsible for these acts because it placed the supervisor in the position of authority to act on the employer's behalf. With the *quid pro quo* type of harassment, even if the employer enforces a policy against the granting of employment benefits on the receipt of sexual favors, any supervisor who grants or refuses to grant entitled employment benefits because of sexual favors will expose the employer to liability for the supervisor's actions.

The issue of employer liability in "hostile work environment" sexual harassment is more complex. If the company knew or should have known that such acts were occurring and did nothing to cure the situation, it may be held liable because it will be seen as condoning this behavior. If, however, it took what the law sees as "reasonable measures" to prevent such conduct and the conduct was not brought to its attention, then it may be protected from liability. The argument is that an employer cannot approve of behavior it does not know about. These are complex issues, but individuals who are thinking about bringing a sexual harassment complaint should be aware of them.

The filing of the initial complaint should be against the employer (company) and not the supervisor or co-worker who is the perpetrator.

Remedies: What Title VII Can Do

Before passage of the 1991 Amendment to the Civil Rights Act, the remedies available under Title VII were very limited. If either the EEOC or the victim took the case to court, the most that the court could do was to order the employer to stop engaging in the unlawful employment practice and "order such affirmative action as may be appropriate, which may include, but is not limited to, reinstatement — with or without back pay — or any other equitable relief as the court deems appropriate." The most back pay the victim could receive was "two years prior to the filing of the charge."

Title VII, unlike state law, contained no provisions for awarding victims of sex discrimination damages — money — either for compensation for the harm suffered or for punitive purposes. Punitive damages is additional money awarded to punish the offending party and to discourage others from engaging in such acts. Both compensatory and punitive damages may be awarded to a successful plantiff.

Looking To The Future:

The 1991 Amendment To The Civil Rights Act

In November, 1991, President Bush signed into law the "Civil Rights Act of 1991" which extends the rights available to sexual harassment victims under Title VII.

The most important effect of the 1991 Civil Rights Act, for readers of this handbook, is that it greatly expanded the remedies now available in sexual harassment cases. The

1991 Act specifically states that victims of intentional discrimination may now seek compensatory and punitive damages in addition to the back pay and other remedies previously available. Compensatory damages specifically do not include any back pay which still may be awarded in addition to the compensatory award. Compensatory damages under the 1991 Amendment will be determined based upon such things as emotional pain, suffering, inconvenience, mental anguish, loss of enjoyment of life and other monetary losses as well as potential monetary losses. In addition, the victim may be awarded punitive damages if she can show that her employer acted "with malice or with reckless indifference" to her rights. While compensatory and punitive awards are now available, the 1991 Civil Rights Act has put a cap on the total maximum amount of compensatory plus punitive damages a victim of sexual harassment may recover. The smaller the defendant/company, the lower the cap. The total amount of damages ranges from $50,000 for victims working for companies with between 15 and 100 employees to $300,000 for victims working for companies with more than 500 employees. Intermediate maximums of $100,000 and $200,000 apply to companies with between 101-200 and 201-500 employees, respectively.

In addition, sympathetic members of Congress continue to introduce bills that attempt to address the on-going problem of sexual harassment. One such recently introduced bill, the "Employee Equity and Job Preservation Act," seeks to allow sexual harassment victims to bring complaints under other federal civil rights statutes.

While it is clear that the problem of sexual harassment will not be solved through legislation alone, the sound policy reflected in the laws passed in 1964 and 1991 represents the increasing seriousness with which society is taking this issue. Still, each victim of sexual harassment will probably continue to question whether or not to file a claim. The new public awareness and enlightened cultural climate encourage and support women in taking the risk of coming forward and confronting their harasser. The new law will make it easier to file a claim, increase the possibility of receiving substantial damages, and is designed to afford protection of one's rights under that law. While it is still untested, this new law appears to have teeth and should send a clear message to would-be harassers and employees that unwanted and discriminatory sexual behavior in the workplace can lead to costly consequences.

CASE HISTORY: David

Susan is a 34-year-old divorced stockholder in a major securities brokerage house. David is a 37-year-old married stockbroker in the same firm. David is new to the firm and was hired as a securities consultant. Part of his job responsibilities include working with the individual brokers and training them in specialized areas of securities analysis.

Susan took an immediate liking to David. She found him to be intelligent, attractive, well-dressed and witty. He reminded her of her ex-husband, Paul, whom she had only recently divorced. Susan had met Paul at work and they had begun dating and got married in less than six months. Susan was swept off her feet by Paul's charm and wealth, only to find that his interest in her soon changed to interest in other women. He had taught her that men are fickle, a lesson that she could not forget.

The first time Susan knew she would be meeting with David, she was ready for the occasion. Her dress was suggestive; her manner was inviting. David was seemingly responsive and Susan was sure he was interested. She could tell just by the way he smiled at her that he was available and that they were going to enjoy an excellent "working" relationship.

Susan soon found excuses why her workload required more and more of David's time. Initially he did not object and perhaps even enjoyed her admiration. He was, however, married and, from his point of view, his interest in Susan did not extend beyond their professional relationship. It was also becoming clear to David that whatever Susan had in mind, it was more than he was willing to accommodate. He soon began to act more reserved and their meetings were curtailed to necessary interactions.

Shortly thereafter a number of stockbrokers in the office gathered for lunch and by chance both David and Susan happened to be among them. Since Susan's purpose for attending the luncheon was unclear and her invitation had come late, she was certain that David had arranged to have her join them. She was delighted. In fact, she slipped home to dress up for the occasion, making the excuse that she had spilled coffee on her blouse. At lunch she was determined to sit next to David, even to the extent of pushing aside an associate. She tried to monopolize David's attention and reluctantly allowed him to turn to another colleague for conversation. By the end of lunch Susan was totally enamored of David and was certain that he shared her feelings.

Susan was so elated to finally have had an opportunity for social interaction with David that she felt compelled to let him know how pleased she was that he had arranged to spend time with her. She decided to send him a note, which stated in part:

"So glad that we finally got some time together alone. I know that you arranged this for some time for us to be together. I so enjoy some romance again. Don't worry, our relationship is safe with me."

David was stunned. He was aware that Susan seemed to want to flatter him, but he thought that he had discouraged any improper contact. And certainly he had not arranged the luncheon. David assumed he had inadvertently led her on and planned to apologize for his participation in their misunderstanding.

At the same time Susan was making plans for their affair. Meeting at her apartment was fine with her; the divorce was now final. Perhaps, however, David preferred a hotel. After all, he was still married, at least for now. He spoke little of his wife — they must not be getting along.

At her first opportunity, Susan decided to call David at home. She assumed he would be surprised — if not delighted — to hear from her. After a brief word about a business concern, she turned the conversation to personal matters. David's response was courteous but short and abrupt and the conversation ended quickly. Susan was disappointed that his tone was not more romantic, but, after all, she thought, how can he express romance to her with his wife nearby? Their relationship would have to be nurtured from the office.

David was clearly uncomfortable with Susan's advances and wondered what he might have done to lead her on. He also contemplated what he might do to turn her down. He decided not to confront her, but to respond to her note in a casual manner. He left her a note, advising that he had not arranged the luncheon but was glad that she enjoyed it. He also stated that he did not know what "relationship" she was referring to, but that a friendship would be okay with him.

Susan was elated. After all, she could "read between the lines" and besides, David was perfect for her. She decided to take the initiative and extend the next invitation. She waited for an opportunity to see David alone and invited him to her home for dinner.

His unanticipated response was to become agitated. He explained to Susan that he was married and did not have romantic interest in other women. It was not anything personal, he explained, but he just was not interested.

Susan, however, was convinced that David was right for her and decided not to give up. She continued to seek his attention professionally and sought various opportunities to see him. In the meantime, she found more occasions to call him at home and to engage him in conversation not pertinent to business.

The firm's annual Christmas party provided Susan's next opportunity to see David socially. By the time he arrived, she had been there for some time and had already drunk several cocktails. She whisked David into a corner where she pressed her affections on him. He resisted her advances and immediately left the party. Being partly drunk, Susan did not get what had happened. Lapses in memory were filled in by wishful thoughts so that what she remembered led her to believe that she had begun a relationship. Susan sent David a second note, similar to the first.

Since David was a contract consultant with no permanent job responsibilities, he inquired at the personnel office about being transferred. He was finding it increasingly difficult to function on the job. He was distracted, forgetful and irritable. His energies were spent avoiding Susan rather than doing the tasks needed to succeed on the job.

At this point the telephone calls at home were becoming more frequent and his wife had heard from other colleagues about David's new companion. With trouble at home and no immediate job prospects, David confronted Susan. Agitated and irate, he told her that he did not like being chased around and repeated that he had no romantic interest in her. He was clear and direct and left before she had an opportunity to respond.

Susan was dismayed but not deterred. After all, she thought, everyone has a bad day. David's wife was probably pressuring him and he needed her to be supportive. She resolved to "be there" for him. On her next opportunity to confront David alone, Susan was unusually affectionate with him. Her dress was intentionally revealing and her manner clearly seductive. David was again speechless, unable to think on his feet and unsuspecting of this latest confrontation. He backed away without comment, nervous about who might be watching and agitated about still being pursued.

Before their next confrontation, David was notified that there was in fact a job opening in a branch office in another state. Reluctant to disrupt his life but anxious to escape Susan's advances, David agreed to go.

What Happened?

Two years later, David has settled into his new office and Susan has not attempted to contact him except by letter a few weeks after he left, to which he did not respond. David continues to resent having had to leave his office and still wonders whether he could have chosen another route to end the problem.

Discussion

David's case demonstrates that men as well as women can be the recipients of unwelcome conduct. More specifically, however, this case is presented in order to discuss the issue of sexual harassment resulting from a "hostile work environment." Title VII of the Civil Rights Act of 1964 protects employees from having to work in a sexually offensive or abusive environment.

One of the central questions which needs to be answered in order to determine whether a hostile environment has been established is whether the conduct under question was severe and pervasive enough to actually alter the terms of a person's employment. In making this determination, the unwelcome conduct must be viewed from the victim's perspective. Since most victims are female, this has generally been from the viewpoint of a "reasonable woman." However, in this case it would be viewed from the perspective of a "reasonable man."

Thus, the question is whether Susan's behavior as viewed by David was severe and pervasive enough that a reasonable man would feel that it altered the conditions of his employment and created an abusive and hostile working environment.

It would appear that Susan was experiencing something akin to a "fatal attraction." Regardless of David's demeanor or responsiveness, she persisted in pressing herself on him verbally in writing and physically.

Despite David's letting her know that her conduct was unwelcome, which is very important, Susan persisted and even escalated her calls to his home, disrupting his family life. Her behavior was clearly beginning to affect David's emotional well-being. He began to experience serious difficulty doing his job.

David chose to solve his problems by finding a position with his company in another state. Should he have chosen to file a complaint, he should have had sufficient evidence to support his claim. His ability to function on the job, his family life and his sense of well-being were severely disrupted by Susan's behavior. A reasonable man would find David's reactions to this "fatal attraction" situation quite credible. Most importantly, on more than one occasion and in clear terms, David let Susan know that her behavior was unwelcome and should be stopped.

CHAPTER • FOUR

From The Predictable To The Bizarre: Why Sexual Harassment Occurs

At this point we have discussed what sexual harassment is, how, when and to whom it occurs and the toll it takes on its victims and the organizations that employ them. This chapter will present some ideas about the cultural conditions, the victims and the perpetrators that contribute to the problem of sexual harassment.

Romance In The Office

Today the workplace is a place where men and women meet each other and develop social relationships. As recently as the past five years, organizations have become noticeably more tolerant of dating among co-workers. Whereas even a few years ago most management personnel frowned upon romantic involvement among employees and often imposed their views by negatively influencing the individuals' careers, today most companies accept dating among co-workers (so-called "equals"), finding that it does not affect productivity in the workplace and therefore need not be discouraged.

The reason that romance seems to flourish in the workplace is largely obvious. More and more women are entering the workforce, making it a truly "co-ed" environment. Women are appearing at every level of the organizational ladder, which means that they work at every level with male co-workers and managers. Men and women spend the greatest part of their waking hours in work-related activities. They work closely together, sharing ideas and generating a familiarity with each other, which may eventually lead to some people developing romantic interests in others. This is expected, considering the intensity and closeness of the working relationships.

But even if romance among so-called "equals" is becoming more accepted, both management and workers continue to actively discourage relationships between superiors and their subordinates. These relationships between "unequals" lead to two types of problems.

First, co-workers of the subordinate employee are likely to feel that the relationship gives an unfair advantage to that person, whether true or not. This affects the productivity of the others and takes a heavy toll on the organization. Even if there is no unfair advantage, co-workers may resent the lack of attention directed toward them, which results in an unmotivated work environment for everyone. Even supervisory personnel may feel that one employee is receiving unfair or "special" treatment. They may also believe that their co-worker (the boss) is somehow using the employee or violating the rules of the workplace, thus raising further issues of trust among the management team.

The second type of problem that arises in this context occurs when the romance goes sour, particularly when it is the subordinate who breaks it off. In such cases, the boss may not be used to taking "no" for an answer and may continue to pursue the subordinate (usually female) or may threaten or even retaliate against the rejection, creating the circumstances that contain all the hallmarks of sexual harassment. Under these circumstances it may be almost impossible for her to press any claim of harassment, even if she clearly says that she has had enough.

Many courts believe, and at least one has clearly stated, that a woman who voluntarily chooses to get involved with her boss removes an element of protection that the employment situation otherwise provides and she must assume the consequences of that choice, including negative reactions if and when she terminates the affair. The courts have never said that such a woman does not deserve the protections of the law against sexual harassment, but prevailing in such a case has so far proven to be a surprisingly difficult task. More often than not it is the women who are paying the higher price, economically, emotionally and in terms of their careers. What we are beginning to learn more about is how an office romance, when ended, may turn into a sexual harassment situation.

Given the enormous risks, especially for women, of these types of relationships at work, the question still arises as to why they continue to happen with such frequency. There are probably many reasons. On the most basic level, the absence of publicity has prevented women from learning about the consequences of these potentially devastating experiences. To some extent this is a result of a reluctance of women to speak up, even to each other. Shame, embarrassment, fear and a lack of cultural and personal supports have forced many women not to speak about their experiences and let other women learn from them.

Another apparent reason that these relationships continue to occur is that work has become a significant opportunity for the expression of power in both men and women and that women take part in these relationships because a sexual liaison at work increases their sense of control over their working situation. Often women cannot feel in control in a male-dominated environment unless they are led to believe that they have been granted some special power or privilege. To the extent that these women equate "power" and "control" with "men," they feel the only way to get the power and therefore control is through an intimate and exclusive association with one of these men. In fact, with rare exceptions, these women are not being valued. They are being used and violated.

Other women assume the risk of these relationships merely because of the challenge they pose. They find energy and excitement meeting secretly, sneaking around, and pretending that no one knows, but enjoying the resulting rumors and the fascination of others. The challenge comes both in getting into the relationship and in believing it is being kept secret, even if in fact everyone in the office knows about it. Many a relationship has maintained its excitement through the energy that it takes to cover it up.

In the final analysis, women pay the heavier price for such relationships. A man's reputation is less likely than a woman's to be tarnished by an inappropriate affair at work since society has much less tolerance for the perceived errors of a woman's ways. Women also end up paying a higher price for these relationships because they are usually in the subordinate positions and if the organization must let go of someone because of a relationship that went sour, it is easier and cheaper to let go of the woman. While male supervisors are increasingly being called to task, it is still more risky for a woman to become romantically involved with her boss.

Male/Female Misunderstandings That Can Lead To Harassment

History is filled with jokes, anecdotes and stories of how men and women are different and often misunderstood by each other. Every other day a report appears by a social scientist that documents even further that men and women are different in certain basic ways and often fail to recognize their differences. Can these misunderstandings be responsible for some of the sexual harassment that occurs in the workplace? We are beginning to understand that men and women do, in fact, view and organize their worlds differently and that they bring these perceptions and communications with them to the workplace.

In her book on male and female communications, *You Just Don't Understand,* Deborah Tannen documents numerous situations in which men and women interpret the same conversation or situation very differently. Moreover, they are often never even aware that there was an apparent misunderstanding. Acknowledging this phenomenon, consider the situation of people who meet in the workplace where an attraction begins to build even before they have much time to get to know one another. At this point we are just talking about typical or "normal" men and women and not those who might be classified as disturbed or deviant. What is the likely result? Misunderstandings run rampant merely as a result of misperception and people act on these misunderstandings.

What kind of perceptual, stylistic and communication differences between normal men and women can lead to such misunderstandings? The following is not meant to be a complete analysis of male/female differences, but a basic outline of what these differences are and how they provide a context for unwanted behavior. These are just a few generalizations.

A. Men are from a very early age used to establishing their position in their male group through competition. Men are always competing and competition is at the core of their behavioral style. Women, on the other hand, typically seek to establish a cooperative and nurturing environment in which people work together rather than compete with one another.

B. Men thrive on conflict. Conflict provides them with the opportunity to establish dominance and secure their position in the pecking order or organizational hierarchy. They are concerned with winning. Women, on the other hand, go to great lengths to avoid confrontation and establish a friendly atmosphere. They are more concerned with not hurting others' feelings than with winning.

C. Men are concerned with action and with results. Words are far less important than deeds. Women, on the other hand, need to talk things through, emphasize sharing and discussion and place great stock in the power of words.

D. Men value independence and self-sufficiency. A man's ability to rely only on himself is a part of his competitive nature and is basic to his self-esteem. Doing something on his own sets him apart from other less competent males and secures his position in the pecking order. Women, on the other hand, typically seek collaboration and cooperation. A woman has no problem asking for assistance and might readily approach a co-worker or supervisor, male or female.

E. Men do not typically seek out personal relationships based upon emotional intimacy. Men typically develop two types of relationships with adults. The first is described in (D) above, characterized as competitive, achievement-oriented, conflict-laden and turf-building. This may or may not be friendly in nature but is designed to establish dominance. The second type of relationship is designed to satisfy a man's needs for affection and intimacy, and typically this is accomplished through sexual interaction. Men do not often want to be "just friends" with women. Women, on the other hand, highly value and strive to develop connected, emotionally intimate relationships with both men and women. These relationships, in which they share and process personal thoughts, feelings, desires, experiences, dreams and goals, can be nonsexual in nature and can be developed with a male as well as a female.

F. Probably the most critical difference between men and women is the function that sexual activity plays in their lives. The relationships between a man and other men, primarily one of competition, conflict and achievement, serve to establish superiority. Male relationships with females are primarily dominated by a man's sexual instinct. Men place great importance on female attractiveness, availability, submissiveness and loyalty. They have an over-riding need to express themselves sexually. Conquest, expression and satisfaction of their sexual drive are the primary motivators in men seeking such a relationship.

Women, on the other hand, while certainly being interested in the sexual aspect of a relationship, do not typically view it as the highest priority. Women are more interested in feeling connected to another person. They want a relationship with someone who will respect them and engage them in verbal and emotional exchanges of a personal nature. In this special human connection they also look for the man to offer resources they need in order to connect and nurture. Men typically satisfy their less intense need for connection through their participation in organizations and activities outside of female relationships.

So how can these male/female differences contribute to instances of sexual harassment?

A woman, who is behaving in the workplace in a typical female manner by being friendly, welcoming, cooperative and nurturing, encounters the typical male. Since he relates to and views relationships with women in terms of sexual expression and conquest, he may misinterpret the woman's friendly and welcoming behavior as an invitation for sexual intimacy. Further, since men place greater importance on what one does rather than what one says, he may also believe that if a woman is being warm, friendly and helpful, even if she seems to say no to a sexual relationship, she is probably just being coy or perhaps shy. As a result, he continues to pursue her, interpreting what is happening from his male point of view, focusing on her actions and not believing her words. A typical man may carry his pursuit to the point of harassment if he does not understand the woman's message.

As discussed earlier, women, by their nature, strive to establish connections with other people, male and female. These connections are often nonsexual and give women the feeling of being part of something bigger than themselves, which offers safety, assistance, nurture and support. The work environment, the place where men and women may spend more time than any other, is a place where women seek to establish such connections. Since men tend to make connections with women through sex, the intentions of women trying to establish a nonsexual relationship with a man at work can, and often is, misperceived. The fact that this relationship may be occurring at work is often of little consequence. Again, this is fertile soil for unwanted behavior to develop.

Consider, for example, a woman in the workplace who is trying to complete a project or learn a new task. If she needs assistance, she will probably have no problem asking for it. She values collaboration and sees it as a positive quality that she can ask for help, even from a male supervisor or co-worker. This same man, however, values his independence and would not think of approaching a woman for help unless he had an ulterior motive, i.e., "Let's get together sexually." Since he thinks that this is how all people operate, he may misinterpret her behavior as an attempt to come on to him. He may believe that her motive is not to ask for help, but to let him know that she is available. This can lead to harassment if a contrary message is not clearly given.

What is the woman thinking while the man has a sexual encounter on his mind? She may enjoy his company as a friend but be quite taken aback that he would read something else into the relationship. She may also regret the loss of friendship and the loss of a resource for her learning on the job. Once she becomes aware of his perceptions, however, she may or may not choose to communicate her perspective.

When men are clearly and firmly told that their sexual advances are unwelcome, most men will stop their pursuit. They may feel resentful and perhaps even angry. They may accuse the women of leading them on, but they will stop and the harassment will end. There are, however, a percentage of men, who as a result of their exaggerated male orientation and/or their own psychological deviance, will continue and even escalate their sexual pursuit. Such men are unable or unwilling to accept no as an answer and to do whatever is necessary to achieve their goal, including sexual harassment.

Men Who Cross The Line:
What To Look For And Why

We have seen that sexual harassment can evolve as a result of how men and women perceive common situations differently, and that this can result in misunderstandings. But certainly these misunderstandings cannot account for all cases of harassment, particularly those in which the victim's wishes are clearly expressed. So the next question becomes, why does a man persist in engaging in behavior that is unwelcome? What kind of man manipulates, coerces and threatens a woman in the workplace?

Little research has been done in this area. Since sexual harassment as a legal claim is fairly new and in the past women have been reluctant to file complaints and pursue formal grievances, the opportunities to study its social phenomenon have been very limited. What little information we have has come largely by listening to the stories of women who have come forward and by examining the characteristics of perpetrators of other illegal sexual acts. This has provided some insight into who the sexual harasser is and why he engages in this kind of offensive behavior.

Psychologists typically describe any specific trait or behavior shown by a particular group of people as distributed along a continuum, with people at one end having little of that trait and people at the other having a lot of it. Most people will fall somewhere in the middle and therefore have an average amount of that trait or behavior. This is usually what is referred to as being normal. So what does this mean in terms of sexual harassment? It means that at some point the perpetrators of sexual crimes have crossed over the line from normal, average or typical male behavior to a point where this behavior is exaggerated, distorted or deviant. For example, elsewhere in this book we have described a typical characteristic of men is a basic sexual orientation toward relationships that leads them to interpret certain signals from women as sexual invitation. Thus the average man often interprets female behavior in sexual terms, even if the female does not intend to be communicating a sexual message.

If the typical or normal male acts on his perception, or misperception, and approaches the female sexually, but his approach is unwanted and he is asked to stop, he will, albeit reluctantly, stop. Some men may persist more than others, but given a clear message, most will eventually stop. This represents the large majority of men. The deviant male, on the other hand, may not take the "stop" message as intended. He may interpret it as playing hard to get, teasing or some other form of seduction, control or ridicule on the part of the female. He may, therefore, persist in his unwanted behavior and even escalate his manipulative or threatening approach. The perpetrator of sexual harassment crosses over the line which separates normal from deviant behavior. In the extreme, the deviant male may become what every woman fears the most: physically violent.

Compare the following examples:

Case 1

Sharon began a new job as a secretary in a large corporation, grateful to have a job and eager to do well. Early on she met Chuck, who ran the photocopy room. She was pleasant to him as she tried to be with everyone. However, as time went on and she encountered him frequently, she started to feel uncomfortable, particularly about the way he seemed to look at her. He began to greet her with, "Hi, honey" and refer to her as "sweetie." Soon he started to become more "familiar" and would intentionally brush up against her or otherwise find a reason to touch her. His conversation often upset her as he would talk in sexually explicit terms and look at her as though he were coming on to her. Not wanting to make a fuss, Sharon remained cordial and composed, although trying to appear distant and uninterested. Chuck didn't get the message and Sharon found herself avoiding the photocopy room, but soon realized the situation was interfering with her job. Finally Sharon asked him to stop this behavior. Chuck got angry at her and then accused her of leading him on by smiling and flirting. He did, however, stop the behavior that made Sharon uncomfortable.

Case 2

Susan was working late one night after most of the staff had gone home. She was headed for the ladies' room when her supervisor, Charles, greeted her. On many previous occasions Charles had indicated a social interest in Susan but she had always rebuffed his advances. Susan was cordial and continued on her way. Charles followed her and asked her to step into his office where he told her that he was very attracted to her and felt excited when he was near her. When Susan asked him what he wanted, he replied very calmly that he wanted to have sex with her. He promised that if she agreed, he in turn would guarantee her job security. He also mentioned that the company was considering a number of lay-offs and that she might otherwise be among them. Susan was confused and frightened and felt that she had no alternative. She couldn't afford to lose her job. She agreed reluctantly and right then and there, Charles took advantage of her. This occurred regularly over a period of more than two years until Susan eventually left the company.

Men who cross over the line appear to be less interested in sex than they are in the exercise of power and control.

Sex becomes the means rather than the end. The "end" is the ability to manipulate and control the victim. Men who have the potential to be sexually abusive to women often have two sides to their personalities. One is the part that harbors those qualities relating to their abusive nature, their need to dominate and feel superior to women. They use sex to express their need to manipulate and control while also satisfying their own physical urges. The other side of their personalities is marked by an ability to be deceptively charming and attentive. This is the man who appears admiring, attentive and even caring about a woman.

The following are some danger signals that should alert a woman that she may be dealing with an abusive personality:

1. A man who views women as unequal and inferior may be an abuser. If he believes that women should be submissive, dependent and "know their place," he may try to put them there.

2. A man who makes derogatory comments about women and uses demeaning language when referring to women should be viewed skeptically. This type of man believes he has the right to lead, direct and control women. This is a danger sign for potential abuse.

3. A man who is known to abuse alcohol or illegal drugs should always present reason for caution. Substance abuse often goes hand-in-hand with uncontrolled, aggressive and abusive behavior.

4. A man whose personality is characterized by excessive use of denial and suppressed emotions should be kept at a distance. A person who is out of touch with his true emotions will take little re-

sponsibility for his actions. He will tend to place blame on others or external circumstances and feel justified in his deviant behavior.

5. A man with a low tolerance for frustration and difficulty in dealing with stress is one who may have an excessive need to manipulate and control. A noticeable problem dealing with conflict or disagreement in a calm and rational manner should be viewed as a danger signal. When such a man is unable to prevail he may demonstrate temper tantrums, which in the extreme may involve physically aggressive or violent behavior. Verbally threatening and abusive behavior is not uncommon in this type of personality and is a clear sign of deviance.

Psychologists have attempted to explain why some men have an excessive need to exercise power over women. One position suggests that men grow up being under the power of women — their mothers. If a father is absent or unable to help them deal with their feelings toward women, they may not learn appropriate adaptive responses. For some men these emotions toward women are deeply buried and can lead to "acting out" behavior which can take various deviant forms, including sexual harassment.

Another theory suggests that our culture promotes the suppression of feelings, sensitivity and vulnerability in men so they will be thought of as "real men." These real men do not feel anything. When this suppression is carried to an extreme, a man is unable to feel or experience his own vulnerability. This effectively prevents him from having any understanding or empathy for what a woman might experience when abused or harassed. In the absence of empathy, men treat women as objects because these men cannot feel the pain that their behavior causes. Severely suppressed men, therefore, see no reason to stop their behavior.

A third position is presented by those psychologists who study men in organizations. They describe a process called "ritual wounding." Ritual wounding is part of the male initiation into the society of men and it occurs in hierarchical organizations in which men compete with one another. As part of establishing a position in relation to other men, particularly in terms of a career, men deal with co-workers and superiors very competitively. Being put down, shamed and harassed is all part of the induction into this world.

These men then do the same thing to their subordinates, both men and women, and expect women to respond to "ritual wounding" in the same manner as do men. They do not understand that "ritual wounding" is not part of the female experience and what may be routine behavior to men is experienced as alien and hurtful to women. When this behavior is expressed through sexual innuendo and badgering, it can be viewed as sexual harassment.

As women who are sexually harassed come forward and pursue the legal recourses available to them, the known perpetrators will become greater in number, allowing for a better profile to be drawn and greater understandng of their abusive instincts to develop. The expectation is that while they may have characteristics in common with other types of abusers, there are some unique factors that lead them to express their deviance in this way.

Who Is Likely To Be Victimized: Some General Characteristics

A victim of sexual harassment can be anyone: you, I or the person next to you. The victim can be young or old, single or married, male or female. Usually a woman though, she may or may not be attractive and she may or may not be a willing participant. She only needs to work in an organization whose structure puts her in a position subordinate to someone who has the need, desire and opportunity to take advantage of her. She is even more vulnerable if she is not willing to leave the organization.

Within this broad spectrum there are a number of characteristics that are typical of victims of employment harassment. For example, a victim is usually young, often in her twenties. She is generally not married or is divorced. She probably has some education, but this can range from secretarial skills to professional training.

Victims of harassment are often physically attractive. They are also frequently members of racial or ethnic minorities. This is because some men believe the stereotype of racial and ethnic minority women as being more willing, submissive or accustomed to being dominated by men.

If the victim is a male, he is also more likely to be a member of a minority group. He is also likely to hold a position in the organization that is on the lower end of the pecking order, often a lesser skilled or trainee position.

Victims of harassment are often found in organizations where there is a vastly unequal balance of one sex to the other. This may be because the job is one not typically done by a person of that sex, e.g., male nurses or female FBI agents, or because one sex, usually women, have not yet made inroads in to such positions, e.g., boards of trustees of corporations.

Men and women who appear to be vulnerable and more easily intimidated are good candidates for harassment. Also, people who tend to be more submissive and less prone to fighting for their rights might find themselves victims of harassment. People who really need their current income and cannot afford to lose their job, even temporarily (e.g., a divorced mother of young children) may be particularly vulnerable.

Similarly, people who are in unusual jobs that they are not likely to find elsewhere (e.g., special counsel at the Department of Education in Washington) are often victimized because of their reluctance to risk losing such a position.

Finally, people who are in positions of high stress which generate intense emotions (e.g., a pediatric cancer nurse) are easily taken advantage of and vulnerable to manipulation. In certain types of high stress jobs, people are unable to control what happens to them. Despite great effort, there is simply nothing they can do. The fatigue and frustration which results from these jobs create a sense of intimacy among co-workers and may make them vulnerable to manipulation and abuse.

As mentioned initially, this profile is not intended to be exhaustive and sexual harassment can and does happen to women who have none of the foregoing characteristics. By the same token, many who have more than one of the above are never harassed. Nevertheless, these characteristics are representative of people who may be more likely to become targets of sexual harassment.

Case History: Joanne

It took years of hard work and determination but my life-long dream was about to come true only months before my fortieth birthday. I had wanted to be a corporate big shot and I had wanted to do it in New York. My field is publishing and anyone who is anyone in publishing is in a major clearinghouse in New York. Before my big opportunity to get to the main office in New York, I had had to give up a lot to move up the ladder.

Five years ago, with my biological time clock ticking away, I gave up the chance to marry Mr. Right to take a job in another city. Another Mr. Right never appeared again, probably because my 60 to 70 hour work weeks left little time to even dream about dating. I am not really complaining, though. Sometimes we have to make tough choices in life and I have always done what I thought was right for me.

Two months ago one of the company's giants based in New York announced his early retirement at the end of the year. Although I was clearly qualified for this job, I wouldn't even allow myself to dream about it because I knew the competition would be fierce. Besides this wasn't a job to be "applied" for. It was one for which you had to hope someone high enough up would recommend you.

Shortly after the announcement of the upcoming New York vacancy, the vice president who headed my branch approached me with the news that he wanted to recommend me for the position and began to prime me for the move. I was elated. For days I thought of nothing else and was almost afraid to breathe in fear that something might upset the apple cart.

The branch vice president was a man by the name of Paul in his fifties with whom I was acquainted but for all intents and purposes I did not really know. We had never worked together and our paths rarely crossed. Apparently, though, he had taken a liking to me and was willing to help me.

After Paul made it known that I would be recommended by our branch for the promotion, he and I had frequent contact. As he put it, there were many things about the business I had to learn in a short period of time — and he would have to teach me. I was so flattered and grateful for this opportunity that I didn't immediately realize that his interest in me was peculiar. For example, I thought nothing of his wanting to take me to lunch until it seemed to become a regular commitment. Later it became dinner, evenings and weekend work days which was not unusual in terms of hours, but was beginning to feel oppressive. Nevertheless, I was afraid to rock the boat so I never turned him down.

Within a matter of two weeks, Paul's interest in me had clearly become social and seemingly romantic. I learned that he was 58 years old and divorced. I can't really describe to you how I felt about him. I didn't feel anything. I was grateful for his help, but that was all.

As time went on our working relationship became increasingly social and Paul pressured me for more intimacy. I wasn't the least bit interested in him that way, but I was afraid to resist. I was also afraid to talk about it with anyone as I thought it might risk my current position as well as the promotion. I figured that it was only for a short period of time and I could keep it under control.

I was wrong. Paul began spending long periods of time in my office, asking a lot of personal questions that I did not really want to answer. He also persisted in wanting to work evenings and although I kept making excuses, he kept asking. One Saturday when I told him I had other plans, he really pressured me to change them, insisting that if I wanted this promotion, we had a lot of ground to cover. Then one evening out of the blue, Paul suggested dinner — not just dinner but room service at the local Holiday Inn. I was tongue-tied and he was persistent. I thought that perhaps reluctance and lack of enthusiasm would speak for itself. It didn't. I was particularly angry because my manner had to make it clear to him that I wasn't a willing participant. In any event, he didn't back off and I didn't say no.

I suppose it is important to add that Paul never threatened my promotion and over the weeks that followed, he always helped me along regardless of whether I agreed to sex. He never forced himself on me, but he knew I was afraid to say no. And he was right.

What Happened?

Joanne ultimately did not get the New York position. She was recommended by Paul but a candidate from a different branch was selected. Joanne terminated her relationship with Paul and thereafter he continued to support her professionally.

Discussion

Joanne's case demonstrates a situation in which there is consensual sex between an employee and her superior. While Joanne was not sexually attracted to Paul, she voluntarily had a sexual relationship with him in order to move ahead in her career. The relationship was initiated by the supervisor and job benefits were promised in return for sexual favors. Joanne was never threatened physically or emotionally and her job was never in jeopardy. Thus, despite the fact that a man in a powerful position persistently pursued and engaged in a sexual relationship with a female employee for which he, in return, promised to promote her career aspirations, this would not be considered sexual harassment. Joanne's participation was voluntary. She never clearly told him that his conduct was unwanted and should be stopped. Her well-being or her job were never threatened and, since she did not get the coveted promotion, no one else was exposed to sex discrimination.

CHAPTER • FIVE

Looking Back: How Far Have We Come?

Throughout history men have sought to demonstrate their power and exercise control within their surroundings. At one time dominance was established by physical strength so that the biggest and strongest men became the most powerful. And, of course, since women were naturally smaller than men, their place within the hierarchy was never even questioned.

Gradually, family background replaced physical strength as the source of dominance — a man's place in the world was a function of who his family was, primarily his father. A man's worth was reflected in access to his family's wealth which he would eventually inherit. But again the issue was really neither stature nor money, but the ability to use those things to establish power and control within the environment. And again women had little place in the hierarchy.

Today, history has evolved further; now the workplace has become the arena and men rely upon their intellectual abilities to establish their place in the world. Not surprisingly, the goal is again power and the pecking order is created within the organizational hierarchy. Chapter 4 suggested some ways that men react to this structure, including their struggle to redefine their place through competition and achievement.

But why sexual harassment? Once again, the need to dominate, control and exert power over others is the driving force. Now the entry of large numbers of women into the workforce, along with their relatively low position in the organizational structure, has created perfect new targets for male dominance. Sexual harassment is merely one form of male dominance. It is an opportunity to exercise power and control over someone who is lower in the pecking order. It is no accident that men express their need for power in this way when women are in the picture. It is consistent with the male view of women as objects for the fulfillment of their sexual needs. For a long time women never questioned their participation. They simply accepted that it was the price they had to pay to work in a male-dominated world.

Today, women not only rebel against the situation, but they are also challenging the premise that men must necessarily dominate in the hierarchy. We are also finding out that given the opportunity, women may enjoy the ability to wield power and influence the world they live (and work) in — and they, too, can occasionally perpetrate sexual harassment. But even though women now occupy positions of power, a vastly disproportionate number of men are still responsible for most of the sexual harassment. Thus, although harassment is an expression of power and dominance, it is also a predominantly male form of expression, consistent with men's instinctual need to express themselves in terms of their sexuality.

Through the combined action of enlightened organizations and courageous women, the problem of sexual harassment has come to the attention of the public and is no longer a tightly guarded secret. While it may be naive to think that this problem can be totally eliminated, it is not unrealistic to believe that sexual harassment against individuals and organizations can be significantly reduced through education, sound policies and procedures and commitment by organizations, both private and public, to speedy and just recourse.

APPENDIX A

A Note On Sexual Harassment: What The Federal Government Says It Is

The Equal Employment Opportunity Commission (EEOC) is a federal agency. Like all agencies, it has the power to issue regulations one of which is something called 29 CFR s 1604.11 — "Guidelines on Discrimination Because of Sex" ("CFR" stands for Code of Federal Regulations). This is the regulation that defines sexual harassment as far as the EEOC is concerned. Numerous other federal departments like the Department of Defense, the Department of Agriculture and so forth, also have their own guidelines regarding sexual harassment.

Essentially, all these "guidelines" say the same thing, and as far as readers of this text are concerned (unless they work for one of the several large federal departments with their own guidelines), the EEOC's guidelines are what they should be looking to for guidance. This is also the regulation that all state employment and/or civil rights and/or human rights agencies will look to and will either adopt as is directly from the EEOC's guidelines or will adopt with even more protective wording regarding the rights of victims of sexual harassment.

The EEOC guidelines are as follows:

> A. Harassment on the basis of sex is a violation of . . . Title VII . . . Unwelcome sexual advances, requests for sexual favors and other verbal or physical conduct of a sexual nature constitute sexual harassment when (1) submission to such conduct is made either explicitly or implicitly a term or condition of an individual's employment, (2) submission to or rejection of such conduct by an individual is used as the basis for employment decisions affecting such individual, or (3) such conduct has the purpose or effect of unreasonably interfering with an individual's work performance or creating an intimidating, hostile, or offensive working environment . . .
>
> B. In determining whether alleged conduct constitutes sexual harassment, the Commission will look at the record as a whole and at the totality of the circumstances, such as the nature of the sexual advances and the context in which the alleged incidents occurred. The determination of the legality of a particular action will be made from the facts, on a case by case basis.
>
> C. An employer, employment agency, joint apprenticeship committee or labor organization . . . is responsible for its acts and those of its agents and supervisory employees with respect to sexual harassment regardless of whether the specific acts complained of were authorized or even forbidden by the employer and regardless of whether the employer knew or should have known of their occurrence. The Commission will examine the circumstances of the particular employment relationship and the job functions performed by the individual in determining whether an individual acts in either a supervisory or agency capacity.

D. With respect to conduct between fellow employees, an employer is responsible for acts of sexual harassment in the workplace where the employer (or its agents or supervisory employees) knows or should have known of the conduct, unless it can show that it took immediate and appropriate corrective action.

E. An employer may also be responsible for the acts of non-employees, with respect to sexual harassment of employees in the workplace, where the employer (or its agents or supervisory employees) knows or should have known of the conduct and fails to take immediate and appropriate corrective action. In reviewing these cases, the Commission will consider the extent of the employer's control and any other legal responsibility which the employer may have with respect to the conduct of such non-employees.

F. Prevention is the best tool for the elimination of sexual harassment. An employer should take all steps necessary to prevent sexual harassment from occurring, such as affirmatively raising the subject, expressing strong disapproval, developing appropriate sanctions, informing employees of their right to raise and how to raise the issue of harassment . . . and developing methods to sensitize all concerned.

G. *Other related practices:* Where employment opportunities or benefits are granted because of an individual's submission to the employer's sexual advances or requests for sexual favors, the employer may be held liable for unlawful sex discrimination against other persons who were qualified for but denied that employment opportunity or benefit.

APPENDIX B

Resources

Equal Employment Opportunity Commission
Albuquerque Area Office
505 Marquette, N.W., Suite 1105
Albuquerque, New Mexico 87102-2189
Telephone: (505) 766-2061

Equal Employment Opportunity Commission
Atlanta District Office
75 Piedmont Avenue, N.E., Suite 1100
Atlanta, Georgia 30335
Telephone: (404) 331-6093

Equal Employment Opportunity Commission
Baltimore District Office
111 Market Place, Suite 4000
Baltimore, Maryland 21202
Telephone: (301) 962-3932

Equal Employment Opportunity Commission
Birmingham District Office
1900 Third Avenue, North, Suite 101
Birmingham, Alabama 35203
Telephone: (205) 731-0082

Equal Employment Opportunity Commission
Boston Area Office
1 Congress Street, Room 1001
Boston, Massachusetts 02114
Telephone: (617) 565-3200

Equal Employment Opportunity Commission
Buffalo Local Office
28 Church Street, Room 301
Buffalo, New York 14202
Telephone: (716) 846-4441

Equal Employment Opportunity Commission
Charlotte District Office
5500 Central Avenue
Charlotte, North Carolina 28212
Telephone: (704) 567-7100

Equal Employment Opportunity Commission
Chicago District Office
536 South Clark Street, Room 930-A
Chicago, Illinois 60605
Telephone: (312) 353-2713

Equal Employment Opportunity Commission
Cincinnati Area Office
The Ameritrust Building
525 Vine Street, Suite 810
Cincinnati, Ohio 45202
Telephone: (513) 684-2851

Equal Employment Opportunity Commission
Cleveland District Office
1375 Euclid Avenue, Room 600
Cleveland, Ohio 44115
Telephone: (216) 522-2001

Equal Employment Opportunity Commission
Dallas District Office
8303 Elmbrook Drive
Dallas, Texas 75247
Telephone: (214) 767-7015

Equal Employment Opportunity Commission
Denver District Office
1845 Sherman Street, Second Floor
Denver, Colorado 80203
Telephone: (303) 866-1300

Equal Employment Opportunity Commission
Detroit District Office
477 Michigan Avenue, Room 1540
Detroit, Michigan 48226
Telephone: (313) 226-7636

Equal Employment Opportunity Commission
El Paso Area Office
The Commons Building C., Suite 103
4171 N. Mesa Street
El Paso, Texas 79902
Telephone: (915) 534-6550

Equal Employment Opportunity Commission
Fresno Local Office
1313 P Street, Suite 103
Fresno, California 93721
Telephone: (209) 487-5793

Equal Employment Opportunity Commission
Greensboro Local Office
324 West Market Street, Room B-27
Post Office Box 3363
Greensboro, North Carolina 27401
Telephone: (919) 333-5174

Equal Employment Opportunity Commission
Greenville Local Office
15 South Main Street, Suite 530
Greenville, South Carolina 29601
Telephone: (803) 241-4400

Equal Employment Opportunity Commission
Honolulu Local Office
677 Ala Moana Blvd., Suite 404
Honolulu, Hawaii 96813
Telephone: (808) 541-3120

Equal Employment Opportunity Commission
Houston District Office
1919 Smith Street, 7th Floor
Houston, Texas 77002
Telephone: (713) 653-3320

Equal Employment Opportunity Commission
Indianapolis District Office
46 East Ohio Street, Room 456
Indianapolis, Indiana 46204
Telephone: (317) 226-7212

Equal Employment Opportunity Commission
Jackson Area Office
Cross Roads Building Complex
207 West Amite Street
Jackson, Mississippi 39201
Telephone: (601) 965-4537

Equal Employment Opportunity Commission
Kansas City Area Office
911 Walnut Street, Tenth Floor
Kansas City, Missouri 64106
Telephone: (816) 426-5773

Equal Employment Opportunity Commission
Little Rock Area Office
320 West Capitol Avenue, Suite 621
Little Rock, Arkansas 72201
Telephone: (501) 324-5060

Equal Employment Opportunity Commission
Los Angeles District Office
3660 Wilshire Boulevard, Fifth Floor
Los Angeles, California 90010
Telephone: (213) 251-7278

Equal Employment Opportunity Commission
Louisville Area Office
600 Martin Luther King Jr. Place, Room 268
Louisville, Kentucky 40202
Telephone: (502) 582-6082

Equal Employment Opportunity Commission
Memphis District Office
1407 Union Avenue, Suite 621
Memphis, Tennessee 38104
Telephone: (901) 722-2617

Equal Employment Opportunity Commission
Miami District Office
1 Northeast First Street, Sixth Floor
Miami, Florida 33132
Telephone: (305) 536-4491

Equal Employment Opportunity Commission
Milwaukee District Office
310 West Wisconsin Avenue, Suite 800
Milwaukee, Wisconsin 53203
Telephone: (414) 297-1111

Equal Employment Opportunity Commission
Minneapolis Local Office
220 Second Street South, Room 108
Minneapolis, Minnesota 55401-2141
Telephone: (612) 370-3330

Equal Employment Opportunity Commission
Nashville Area Office
50 Vantage Way, Suite 202
Nashville, Tennessee 37228
Telephone: (615) 736-5820

Equal Employment Opportunity Commission
Newark Area Office
60 Park Place, Room 301
Newark, New Jersey 07102
Telephone: (201) 645-6383

Equal Employment Opportunity Commission
New Orleans District Office
701 Loyola Avenue, Suite 600
New Orleans, Louisiana 70113
Telephone: (504) 589-2329

Equal Employment Opportunity Commission
New York District Office
90 Church Street, Room 1501
New York, New York 10007
Telephone: (212) 264-7161

Equal Employment Opportunity Commission
Norfolk Area Office
252 Monticello Avenue, First Floor
Norfolk, Virginia 23510
Telephone: (804) 441-3470

Equal Employment Opportunity Commission
Oakland Local Office
1333 Broadway, Room 430
Oakland, California 94612
Telephone: (415) 273-7588

Equal Employment Opportunity Commission
Oklahoma City Area Office
531 Couch Drive
Oklahoma City, Oklahoma 73102
Telephone: (405) 231-4911

Equal Employment Opportunity Commission
Philadelphia District Office
1421 Cherry Street, Tenth Floor
Philadelphia, Pennsylvania 19102
Telephone: (215) 656-7020

Equal Employment Opportunity Commission
Phoenix District Office
4520 North Central Avenue, Suite 300
Phoenix, Arizona 85012-1848
Telephone: (602) 640-5000

Equal Employment Opportunity Commission
Pittsburgh Area Office
1000 Liberty Avenue, Room 2038-A
Pittsburgh, Pennsylvania 15222
Telephone: (412) 644-3444

Equal Employment Opportunity Commission
Raleigh Area Office
1309 Annapolis Drive
Raleigh, North Carolina 27608-2129
Telephone: (919) 856-4064

Equal Employment Opportunity Commission
Richmond Area Office
3600 West Broad Street, Room 229
Richmond, Virginia 23230
Telephone: (804) 771-2692

Equal Employment Opportunity Commission
San Antonio District Office
5410 Fredericksburg Rd., Suite 200
San Antonio, Texas 78229
Telephone: (512) 229-4810

Equal Employment Opportunity Commission
San Diego Area Office
880 Front Street, Room 4S-21
San Diego, California 92188
Telephone: (619) 557-6288

Equal Employment Opportunity Commission
San Francisco District Office
901 Market Street, Suite 500
San Francisco, California 94103
Telephone: (415) 744-6500

Equal Employment Opportunity Commission
San Jose Local Office
96 North Third Street, Suite 200
San Jose, California 95112
Telephone: (408) 291-7352

Equal Employment Opportunity Commission
Savannah Local Office
10 Whitaker Street, Suite B
Savannah, Georgia 31401
Telephone: (912) 944-4234

Equal Employment Opportunity Commission
Seattle District Office
2815 Second Avenue, Suite 500
Seattle, Washington 98121
Telephone: (206) 553-0968

Equal Employment Opportunity Commission
St. Louis District Office
625 N. Euclid Street, 5th Floor
St. Louis, Missouri 63108
Telephone: (314) 425-6585

Equal Employment Opportunity Commission
Tampa Area Office
Timberlake Federal Building Annex
501 East Polk Street, Suite 1020
Tampa, Florida 33602
Telephone: (813) 228-2310

Equal Employment Opportunity Commission
Washington Field Office
1400 L Street, N.W., Suite 200
Washington, D.C. 20005
Telephone: (202) 275-7377

REFERENCES

Abby, A. 1982. "Sex Differences In Attributions For Family Behavior: Do Males Misperceive Females' Friendliness?" *Journal of Personality and Social Psychology,* 42:830-838.

Abby, A. and Melby, C. 1986. "The Effects of Nonverbal Cues of Gender Differences in Perception of Sexual Intent." *Sex Roles,* 15:283-298.

Baker, Donghors D., Terpstra, David E. and Lavntz, Kinley. 1990. "The Influence of Individual Characteristics and Severity of Harassing Behavior on Reactions to Sexual Harassment." *Sex Roles,* no. 5/6, 22:305-321.

Collins, E.G.C. and Blodgett, T.B. 1981. "Sexual Harassment: Some See It . . . And Some Don't." *Harvard Business Review,* March/April (79-95).

Connolly, Walter B. Jr. and Marshall, Allison, B. 1989. "Sexual Harassment of University or College Students by Faculty Members." *Journal of College and University Law,* no. 4, 15:381-403.

Dziech, B.W. and Weiner, L. **The Lecherous Professor: Sexual Harassment On Campus.** Beacon Press, Boston: 1984.

EEOC: Policy Guidance On Employer Liability For Sexual Favoritism. The Bureau of National Affairs, Inc. *Daily Labor Report,* Feb. 15, 1990.

EEOC: Policy Guidance On Sexual Harassment. Fair Employment Practices. The Bureau of National Affairs, Inc., no. 645, 405:6681-6701.

Ellison v. Brady, 924 F.2d 872 (9th Cir. 1991).

Farley, L. **Sexual Shakedown: The Sexual Harassment of Women On The Job.** McGraw Hill, NY: 1978.

Gibbs, Nancy. 1991. "Office Crimes." *Time,* no. 15, 138:52-64.

Gorman, Christine. "Sizing Up The Sexes." *Time,* Jan. 20, 1992 (42-51).

Grauerholz, Elizabeth. 1989. "Sexual Harassment of Women Professors by Students: Exploring The Dynamics of Power, Authority, and Gender in a University Setting." *Sex Rules,* no. 11/12, 21:789-801.

Gutek, B., **Sex And The Workplace.** Jossey-Bass Publishers, CA: 1985.

MacKinnon, Catherine A. **Sexual Harassment Of The Working Woman: A Case Of Sex Discrimination.** Yale University Press, CT: 1979.

Malovich, Natalie J. and Stake, Jayne E. 1990 "Sexual Harassment On Campus." *Psychology of Women Quarterly,* 14:63-81.

Masi, Dale A. and Etzioni, David. 1991. "Sexual Harassment And The Role Of EAP Programs." *Employee Assistance,* no. 5, 4:6.

May, S. Beville. 1988. "Sexual Harassment Law In Massachusetts: Where We Stand and Where We Are Headed." *Massachusetts Law Review,* Summer, 60-64.

McKinney, Kathleen. 1990. "Sexual Harassment of University Faculty by Colleagues and Students." *Sex Rules,* no. 7/8, 23:421-437.

Meritor Savings Bank. *FSB vs. Vinson,* 477 U.S. 57, 106 S. Ct. 2399, 91 L.Ed. 49 (1983).

"The Price Of Saying No." *People Weekly.* Oct. 28, 1991, no. 16, 36:44-50.

Player, Mark A. **Employment Discrimination Law.** West Publishing Co., MN: 1988.

Rapp, Ellen. "Dangerous Liaisons." *Working Woman,* Feb. 1992, 56-61.

Riger, Stephanie. 1991. "Gender Dilemmas in Sexual Harassment Policies and Procedures." *American Psychologist,* no. 5, 46:497-505.

Saal, Frank E., Johnson, Catherine B. and Welsor, Nancy. 1989. "Friendly or Sexy?" *Psychology of Women Quarterly,* 13:263-267.

Schneider, Ronna Greff. 1987. "Sexual Harassment and Higher Education." *Texas Law Review,* 65:525-583.

Smolone, Jill. 1991. "She Said, He Said." *Time,* no. 15, 138:36-40.

Statman, Jan Berliner. **The Battered Woman's Survival Guide: Breaking The Cycle.** Taylor Publishing Co., TX: 1990.

Strebeigh, Fred. "Defining Law On The Feminist Frontier." *New York Times Magazine,* Oct. 6, 1991, 25.

Tanner, Deborah. **You Just Don't Understand.** Valentine Books, NY: 1988.

Terpstra, David E., and Baker, Douglas D. 1987. "A Hierarchy of Sexual Harassment." *The Journal of Psychology,* no. 6, 121:599-605.

ABOUT THE AUTHORS

Joel Friedman, Ph.D, is a licensed psychologist in Massachusetts. For the past twenty years he has served on the teaching faculty of the Harvard Medical School and was recently honored for twenty years of service at Massachusetts General Hospital. He has served on the staffs of several Massachusetts hospitals and universities. As president of Bay State Psychological Associates for over nine years, his functions included consultation to a range of institutions from local schools to major national corporations. His private practice has dealt with a wide range of sexual abuse issues including sexual harassment and his writings, which include *Women and the Law* and *Law and Gender Bias* (Fred B. Rothman & Co.), focus on discrimination of women. Dr. Friedman maintains a clinical practice in Brookline, Massachusetts.

Marcia Mobilia Boumil, J.D., LL.M., has taught law for a number of years at Boston College and Suffolk law schools and Tufts University Medical School in Boston where she is currently an Assistant Professor of Community Health. She holds graduate degrees in public health and psychology as well as law and specializes in the field of health and women's issues. She is the author of numerous articles and three books, of which the latest is the legal text, *Women and the Law* (Fred B. Rothman & Co., 1992). Also forthcoming is *Law and Gender Bias*. In addition to her writings on this subject, she has lectured in the field of sexual harassment and other women's issues pertaining to gender discrimination.

Barbara Ewert Taylor, J.D., is a practicing attorney in Massachuetts specializing in the field of civil rights and employment litigation. She has a particular interest in sexual harassment and other forms of sex discrimination and has researched extensively and written in this field. Her publications include the forthcoming book, *Law and Gender Bias,* in which she focuses on sex discrimination in employment.

Other Books By . . . Health Communications

ADULT CHILDREN OF ALCOHOLICS (Expanded)
Janet Woititz
Over a year on *The New York Times* Best-Seller list, this book is the primer on Adult Children of Alcoholics.
ISBN 1-55874-112-7 $8.95

STRUGGLE FOR INTIMACY
Janet Woititz
Another best-seller, this book gives insightful advice on learning to love more fully.
ISBN 0-932194-25-7 $6.95

BRADSHAW ON: THE FAMILY: A Revolutionary Way of Self-Discovery
John Bradshaw
The host of the nationally televised series of the same name shows us how families can be healed and individuals can realize full potential.
ISBN 0-932194-54-0 $9.95

HEALING THE SHAME THAT BINDS YOU
John Bradshaw
This important book shows how toxic shame is the core problem in our compulsions and offers new techniques of recovery vital to all of us.
ISBN 0-932194-86-9 $9.95

HEALING THE CHILD WITHIN: Discovery and Recovery for Adult Children of Dysfunctional Families — Charles Whitfield, M.D.
Dr. Whitfield defines, describes and discovers how we can reach our Child Within to heal and nurture our woundedness.
ISBN 0-932194-40-0 $8.95

A GIFT TO MYSELF: A Personal Guide To Healing My Child Within
Charles L. Whitfield, M.D.
Dr. Whitfield provides practical guidelines and methods to work through the pain and confusion of being an Adult Child of a dysfunctional family.
ISBN 1-55874-042-2 $11.95

HEALING TOGETHER: A Guide To Intimacy And Recovery For Co-dependent Couples — Wayne Kritsberg, M.A.
This is a practical book that tells the reader why he or she gets into dysfunctional and painful relationships, and then gives a concrete course of action on how to move the relationship toward health.
ISBN 1-55784-053-8 $8.95

3201 S.W. 15th Street,
Deerfield Beach, FL 33442-8190
1-800-441-5569

Health Communications, Inc.®

NURTURE YOUR BODY AND SOUL WITH *Changes*

The Nation's Leading Personal Growth Magazine!

CHANGES is the only national self-help magazine that keeps you informed about the latest and best in personal growth and recovery. It brings you valuable insights that will help bring healing and wholeness into the most significant areas in your life.

★ Relationships ★ Mental, physical and emotional wellness
★ Self-esteem ★ Spiritual growth

Each issue of CHANGES features the best, most inspirational writers and thinkers of our time — articles and interviews with authors like J. Keith Miller, John Bradshaw, Nathaniel Branden, Janet Woititz and others who give the gift of self-understanding to millions of people.

CHANGES brings you practical ways to apply the positive, life-affirming philosophy of recovery to family life and friendships, to schools and the workplace, to the changing world around us.

Let CHANGES help you make positive, effective changes to enhance *your* world. A one-year subscription is just $18* for six bi-monthly issues. Plus, you'll receive lots of valuable book, conference and local seminar information.

Subscribe today by mailing the coupon below, or call us toll-free:
1-800-441-5569
and give the operator this number: HCJM72

Clip this coupon and mail it to:
CHANGES Magazine, Subscriber Services, 3201 S.W. 15th Street, Deerfield Beach, FL 33442-8190.

☐ **YES**, enter my subscription to CHANGES for just $18*/year.

Name: _____
Address: _____
City: _____ State: ___ Zip: _____

HCJM72

☐ Payment enclosed ☐ Bill me Charge my: ☐ VISA ☐ MC Exp. Date: _____

Signature: _____ Card #: _____

Please allow 4-6 weeks for your first issue.
*Florida residents add 6% sales tax. For Canadian and Foreign orders, add $20 for postage.